Praise for

Momoir

"Alyssa's first book perfectly captures the warring emotions of becoming a new parent. Her raw honesty and relatable humor make this collection of essays a salve to the young mom's soul."

—Kary Oberbrunner
Author of *Your Secret Name* and *Unhackable*

"God loves us for who we are, not for what we do. That's the good news at the heart of Alyssa DeRose's *Momoir*, an honest, funny and faithful account of perfectly imperfect motherhood."

—Henry G. Brinton
Pastor and author of *City of Peace*

"I'm a sucker for stories of motherhood and in *Momoir*, Alyssa has given us a peek into her journal from her earliest days. As the kids get older and childhood fades, what a gift this is, her experiences recorded while the smell of baby diarrhea is still fresh. For any new mom who wants to feel like she's not alone, for any old mom like me, remembering those hopeful, beautiful, excruciating days postpartum, or for anyone who's ever struggled with the exhaustion and uncertainty of new motherhood, you have a friend in Alyssa. Breathe a sigh of relief that someone's right there with you in the sleeplessness and second guessing."

—Melanie Dale
Author of *Calm the H*ck Down: How to Let Go and Lighten Up about Parenting*

Momoir:

*A New Mom's Journey to Embracing
Her Not-So-Perfect Motherhood*

by Alyssa DeRose

ISBN 978-1-64663-044-8

Cover design by Micah Kandros.

Published by

◄ köehlerbooks™

3705 Shore Drive
Virginia Beach, VA 23455
800–435–4811
www.koehlerbooks.com

Memoir

A NEW MOM'S JOURNEY
TO EMBRACING HER
NOT-SO-PERFECT MOTHERHOOD

ALYSSA
DEROSE

VIRGINIA BEACH
CAPE CHARLES

Table of Contents

To my boys.
No words can do my love justice.

Introduction

I See You, Mama

I wrote most of this book in three places: a donut shop, a gym locker room, and a library.

The donut shop was within walking distance of our Chicago row house and served great coffee for under two bucks—and whilst I was knocked up, excellent cherry Danishes. It had a little room off to the side with fast and free Wifi (too often mutually exclusive in my experience), and they played music from the '40s and '50s—childhood classics for most of my fellow patrons. While my senior compatriots hummed along, sipped small black coffees, and paged through their paper newspapers, I plugged in my earbuds, chugged my large with cream, and clicked away on my MacBook Air. As weeks turned to months, we would offer each other nods as we settled into our morning routines, finding the familiar in a stranger from a different generation. Thank you, Dinkel's, for giving me a sanctuary to start this dream.

The gym locker room makes no sense until you realize that I was provided two precious hours of childcare daily as part of our family membership at our fitness club in the city. A full-time, exhausted stay-at-home mom with a knack for resourcefulness, I would drop Micah off, sneak in a hurried sweat session while mapping out my next essay, and then plug in my laptop in the back corner of the women's locker room. I found it quite easy to ignore the subtle scent of stinky feet as I drank a sparkling water and allowed the drone of the hair dryers to pull me into my work.

I finished the second half of this book from a leather chair with a window view at our new suburban library: probably the likeliest of locales for an aspiring author. Anxious to finish this book once and for all, whenever my husband volunteered to take charge I would steer through the drive-thru and snag a cup of Dunkin' on my way to my personal writing retreat. A creature of habit, I became accustomed to working across from a young man in sweatpants who appreciated working shoeless. Admiring his self-confidence and attendance record, I would join him in tucking up my feet *sans* sneakers whenever we were working at the library. I'm still not sure what he was doing there every day—I found he wasn't much for small talk—but I did catch a glimpse or two of what appeared to be video games on his screen. I'd like to give him the benefit of the doubt and assume he was a computer programmer who preferred a public workspace as opposed to his parents' basement.

I kid, I kid.

I share all this to tell you that there is nothing glamorous about writing a book—or computer programming, apparently.

At least not for me.

Deciding to write this book was not fast or free. It was birthed from a two-year process of carving out little moments in unexpected places at the cost of paid childcare or my husband's productive workday. As I typed this book, word by word and tear by tear, I gave it everything I had. I laid my shame before you. I confessed my fears. I shared my most intimate joys. I hoped it would generate a few laughs.

And I wondered if anyone would ever see these pages printed.

Yet this book exists because I was answering a call from my deepest self, a longing that wouldn't quiet no matter how hard I tried to ignore it. I knew my rocky start to early motherhood was not unique, but my desire to share it openly was. And I believed there were women who needed to hear the sacred words: you are not alone.

You are not failing.

It's okay to struggle.

You are deeply loved.

Writing this book has revealed the beauty in the struggle—my unexpected struggle with motherhood. For me, becoming a mother hasn't been pretty or natural or perfect. I have failed and fallen, and I've wanted to quit more than most. And my faith has been tested along with my sanity.

And there have been so many tears. Just ask my husband.

Journeying back through the words, reliving some of my life's hardest moments, I'm finding that grace is being revealed. In hindsight, I can see how the Lord—and the people who loved me most—walked with me through the many valleys in my story of becoming a mom, even when I was convinced I was all alone.

Similarly, I hope that as you turn the pages of this book, and while encountering my imperfect motherhood with each chapter, you will feel a little more known and a lot less alone.

I see you, Mama.

We can do this.

PART ONE: BECOMING

The Climb We Fall

I'm wearing yoga pants and old sneakers. My hair is tied back in a low ponytail, and the sun is beating down on my bare shoulders. Sweat runs down the middle of my back, and I wonder if that natural deodorant I convinced myself to convert to is up to the job.

Unlikely.

I look upward and all I see is the incline—jarring and infinite. I bear-crawl, struggling to find my footing with each labored step. As I try to gather forward momentum, the dirt gives way underfoot; I slide backward a bit more each time. I'm convinced this is a game of one step forward and two steps back. There must be a way to make this look more graceful!

As the reality sets in that my efforts are futile, I claw the fresh dirt in manic desperation; I can tell I'm getting nowhere. My breath is strained, my lungs burn, and I can feel that metallic taste in the back of my throat that brings back nightmares of running the mile in middle school. Just like back then, when I had to suffer through that god-awful annual reminder that endurance sports are not for me, my entire identity now hangs in the balance:

I must prove that I can do this.

I must be able to make this climb. (I must be able to break the seven-minute-mile record.) I must enjoy this challenge. (Don't forget to put a smile on your face. Make this seem easy, like it is for the other girls.) Don't sweat through your t-shirt.

And most importantly, don't throw up.

You were made for this, weren't you?

Suddenly, Dan appears on my left and puts a strong, firm hand on my shoulder. He tells me to stop, take a breath, and he shows me to a flat rock where I can rest my weary body and soul.

Phew, I didn't puke. Thank God. We did it.

Once I'm settled, he hands me a glass of cucumber water and I take a deep gulp, thankful for a husband who brings me spa water in the middle of a mountain. If only he had remembered to pack some of those dark-chocolate-covered peanut butter cups from Trader Joe's that I love; I live for those things. He did bring an apple, though, which probably makes more sense given the occasion. He's always so prepared for these things.

Just as I'm starting to feel a bit better and I've scarfed down my nutritious snack, he tells me he has to go and starts walking downward and out of sight. He manages to look up towards me a couple of times and offer the kind of smile that makes you think a smile could actually say, "I'm sorry." I lose sight of him, the rock disappears, and I am again left alone. Just me, the wild incline, and a suspicious hankering for dessert.

I lift my head towards the challenge and shield my eyes from the sun. Then I put my hands on my hips, inhale deeply, and get back to work.

Again.

This time there's no snack-bearing husband, and this time it starts to rain—cold rain. Pelting against my body. Just like that time we tried to climb Machu Picchu like real mountain climbers, I want to die and give up. I want to ask a Sherpa to come carry me and all my luggage, or in this case, baggage. But there's no Sherpa, either.

There's just me. This mountain. And my God.

My body aches, and my heart sinks because I don't see a top to this peak. How much time has passed, anyway? I cry out until there's nothing left. The tears stream down my face, and somehow they blend into the river the rain is making around me. When did the mud and rocks completely surrender to the weather? They're tumbling down around me, and I can't keep hold any longer. I can't find my footing. There is nothing to grab.

And just like that, I'm falling.

Falling.

Falling.

Falling.

I wake up with a cold start and grab my phone. I hold it against my nose and close one eye so I can make out the number on the clock. It's 4:00 AM. The baby is crying.

Again.

I feel around blindly for my glasses—a well-practiced habit since the ripe age of four—and grab my water bottle. I make the short, well-worn shuffle to the nursery and lift my wailing son from his crib. We settle into our chair and he hungrily latches onto my body. He sighs with relief as he literally sucks the life out of me. I sit in this chair for the thousandth, no millionth, time—the demands of a twenty-pound human becoming the weight of the world.

And as his crying quiets, mine slowly begins. The tears stream softly down my cheeks, but I make sure not to let him see my emotions. I turn off the light next to me. I take in the darkness and I hold my son.

Another night. The same mountain.

Thankfully, tears don't leave scars in their tracks.

•••••••••••

Four years ago, I was introduced to mountain climbing with the gusto only blissful ignorance can bring. My boyfriend and I had heard Peru was the next "it" spot for adventurers to vacation, and we'd just reached that time in every adult semi-serious relationship where you need to take a trip together to see if this other human could actually be a possibility for the real trip of a lifetime: marriage.

So we got a few tips from friends who'd gone before us, found a tour company, and booked a few flights. Next thing I knew, we had 45-pound packs strapped to our backs, were the proud temporary owners of a rented tent that smelled like bowling shoes, and were at the complete mercy of a friendly tour guide named *Navidad* ("Call me Christmas!" he said).

Overcome with the excitement that only two twenty-somethings on their first big trip together could possess, we set out for our first day of the climb with big smiles and a good amount of ignorance— drastically underestimating the challenges that lay ahead.

Can you say "rookies"?

Four days later, three of them raining (no wonder we paid a great seasonal rate), we had climbed 8,000 feet, had to poop outdoors, and we'd had zero showers.

But we had made it.

Barely.

On our long flight home, we agreed the views had been incredible, worth our blistered feet and possibly even our public defecation. Upon arrival in Chicago, we managed to put that literal shit show behind us and continued to love each other in spite of our newly-lost hygiene secrets.

We had made it.

And a couple years later, on the cusp of our first wedding anniversary, a pair of tiny pink lines announced that a new peak stood before us. Overcome with the excitement only two newlyweds expecting their first child could possess, we shared our news with big smiles and a good amount of ignorance—drastically underestimating the challenges that lay ahead.

Can you say "rookies"?

Just like our trip to Peru, becoming a mom was a mountain for which I was wholly unprepared.

The question was: *would the views be worth the climb?*

Summer

Loss

I'm obsessed with Amazon Prime. I don't see the point in running any errands that can be just as easily accomplished from the comfort of my couch during an evening's marathon of dramatic television. (Much to my husband's chagrin.) Which only partially explains how I end up with a jumbo pack of cheap pregnancy tests under my bathroom sink "just in case" I need them.

You see, toward the end of a four-month European backpacking adventure, after an unfortunate mishap with the airline, our luggage got lost—and our only form of birth control along with it. Now, I'm certain that the Greeks sell contraceptives in their drugstores, but we figured, why not wing things and walk in the way of God's timing for starting a family?

We like to really be prayerful about life's biggest decisions.

So, when I wake up early with an inkling that something might be going on inside my uterus, I bust out that big ol' box o' tests and end up with a dozen or so arranged around the basin of my bathroom sink—each displaying double faint lines.

With my collection of positive pregnancy tests clutched in my shaking hands, I wake Dan up from a dead sleep and show him evidence that our lives are about to turn upside down.

Talk about a wake-up call.

It's hard to explain what happens in those first few moments of hearing this life-changing news. I think we both want to be instantly thrilled, but the better descriptors for our feelings would be "disbelieving" and "overwhelmed." When you're without any physical evidence of a new family member on its way, it's hard to feel like anything's changed, other than a new responsibility to avoid cold cuts, sushi, and wine. And given my penchant for always accepting a glass of my favorite red (or white or rosé or sparkling), I know we'll never make it through the upcoming holiday weekend with our families without blowing our new secret.

So, since we've never been shy about letting our people into our lives, we make the decision that, while our news is literally *brand new* and still in the scary zone, we'll share it with those closest to us and ask for their prayer.

There isn't one person in our inner circle who isn't totally supportive and joyful and loving and prayerful. And we find that, as the outward momentum takes off around us, our excitement begins to catch up. Every night before bed we lie there and say, "Can you believe we're going to be parents?"

And after a couple weeks, we really start to believe it.

So, when we're still a week away from the doctor's appointment where we get to hear the baby's heartbeat (typically eight to ten weeks into pregnancy) and I have some light spotting, we call the office and they have us come in to make sure everything's okay. They start with an ultrasound and a blood test to check my HCG levels (the proof-of-pregnancy hormone) and assure us that since we're only about seven weeks into our pregnancy, the test results and light bleeding are totally normal. The plan is for me to come in a couple more times later in the week for monitoring, and to make sure things continue to develop properly.

But you know that gut feeling you have when something is just not right? Let's just call it a mother's intuition.

I have that feeling.

Later in the afternoon, while napping my terrified emotions away, I awake to severe cramping and know our worst fears are now fact. Over the next two days, my body physically experiences the pain of our hearts breaking. Every time I go to the bathroom, I'm forced to face our new reality all over again, and every time I look at my husband I can't help but cry.

People will tell you that, at seven weeks pregnant, a real baby doesn't exist yet. They'd say this is just my body's way of ridding itself of an embryo that most likely has severe chromosomal abnormalities. But even with the evidence that the baby is just a few cells (barely the size of a blueberry), when your body is losing its ability to keep that blueberry safe, you feel every bit of that loss. The only way I can describe it is that when it's over, there's an emptiness that feels like something that *should be there* is now missing.

It feels like I'm losing a part of my soul. And that's probably because there was another soul sharing my body with me for a short while.

Miscarriage feels like a cruel joke. You go from excitement to heartbreak. From joy to loss. From growing life to losing it. It's basically a horrible oxymoron of a life experience. And throughout this painful week I cry out to God so many times, asking Him "Why?"

Why do You make life just to take it?

Why do we have to be going through this?

Why?

Why?

Why?

I mean, don't You love the little children?

And somehow, alone in the darkness of my pain, I hear Him speak to my battered heart and say, ***"More than you will ever know."***

Even though we don't get to know the "why" behind our pain—and in this broken world we can be sure there will be pain—we do get a free lifelong pass to do life with the only One who can bring us true healing—healing from all the things that hurt us and scar us and utterly shatter us.

We just have to be able to trust Him when it seems like He's just allowed something awful to happen.

Easier said than done, right?

As I slowly come alive again over the next few weeks—mainly through the love and patience of my faithful husband holding my hand and forcing me into quiet moments of prayer and worship with him—you know what I hear God say to my broken heart?

"I am with you."

Because He promises to always be there.

And as I begin to believe Him, over and over again I hear Him whisper, *"I move mountains, Alyssa."*

Because He knows my fears, and He can overcome them. Even if my ever-anxious brain is in a downward spiral of overwhelming worry and despair.

And whenever I think of that little life no longer with me—my heart broken, my soul strangled in grief—He tells me, *"I am taking her with me now; she was not made for this world."*

Because He loves this baby more than I can. And my first child won't know a world with any darkness.

And when all of the doubt about my family's future starts to creep in, He says, *"You will hold a child in your arms."*

Because even in my moments of fear, He gives me hope.

And when my body is done enduring the excruciating process of our loss, I hear Him say, *"Although you have stopped bleeding, I haven't stopped bleeding for you."*

Because *that*, my friends, is the ultimate truth. Our ultimate truth. If He was willing to die for us, doesn't that mean He wants to give us life, too?

While in the midst of the deepest loss of my life, I have no choice but to hope so.

I cling to His truth because I have nothing left in myself. And in the depths of my sadness, I'm met with His presence—in the quiet words He whispers to my broken heart; in the strong arms of my husband, holding me when the pain is too much to bear on my own; through the constant prayers of our people; in the soft worship music that becomes my soul's anthem during these lonely weeks; and by the patient grace of time, which slowly brings me back to life.

When the fog finally lifts and I'm no longer walking around with horror-film-worthy streams of mascara running down my face—who are we kidding, I barely remember mascara—I realize I haven't been this desperate for God in a really long time.

And I'm reminded of the best promise this side of Heaven: *"I will never leave you."*

August

Laughter

It's been several weeks since our miscarriage, and God keeps reminding me of the story of Sarah and Abraham. After a literal lifetime of wanting to be a mother and having to settle for her husband knocking up her maidservant in her place, Sarah heard God announce He was going to give her a child of her own. She was already well beyond child-rearing years and knew it. She probably worried that her ninety-year-old body wouldn't even be able to handle the taxing experience of bearing a child—and with no hope for an epidural!

But my favorite part of this story? When Sarah heard the news from God, she laughed. Even though she'd heard it from the horse's mouth, she still struggled to believe He would give her the desires of her heart. She even tried to lie about her doubt, but God called her out.

Shocker.

I realize that shouldn't be my favorite part of the story, but it makes me feel better to discover I'm not the only one with trust issues, you know?

Thankfully, God remained—and remains—in control. It is written that He was gracious to Sarah, and she bore a son named Isaac at the very time God promised him.

At the very time God promised him.

Isn't that amazing?

In full disclosure, I keep getting mad at Dan for asking God to give us a perfect child in His perfect timing. The control freak in me wants him to pray we'll get pregnant again right away. Immediately. With a perfectly healthy baby. Is that too much to ask?

But what exists in Dan's prayers and subsequently in his heart—that I lack in both of mine—is trust. Trust that God will be gracious to us. Trust that His plans are better than our plans. Trust that He has good promises for our story.

Just like Sarah and Abraham's. I mean, *hello*. Abraham was the father of the promised people. It makes sense for him to have lots of kids, right?

But this anxious heart of mine can be hard to convince. So in my lack of faith, I cling to Dan's confidence. And in my lack of control, I choose surrender.

And in hers, so did Sarah.

When she was finally holding her baby boy Isaac in her arms, Sarah said, "God has brought me laughter, and everyone who hears about this will laugh with me." Isn't that ironic? When she doubted God would ever bring forth her heart's dearest desire, she laughed in disbelief. But when He fulfilled His promise to her—and brought her the very thing she never thought she'd have—He also brought her joyful laughter.

Joyful laughter.

In our hardest seasons in life—when all we can see is loss, death, pain, brokenness—laughter seems impossible. Hopeless. So far beyond our reach.

But what grieving our first child's short life is teaching me is that God remains near, even when the pain is suffocating. He grieves along with us and bears our pain in His hands. He hopes we'll let Him in. He is able to heal our broken hearts. He wants to meet our every need and give us our dearest desires.

He wants us to laugh again.

Laughter may feel like a lifetime away, but if there's one thing our little life has taught my aching heart, it's that *nothing* is impossible with an everlasting and ever-present God.

Not even laughter.

Days Later
Terrifying Months

The proof of our prayers is arranged on our bathroom counter—ten tests boldly proclaiming life, in the form of two parallel lines. Ten tests prove we're being given a second chance at welcoming a child, ten tests that show the results of our love.

TEN tests.

But in a moment that should be defined by joy alone, I let my anxiety take over. I didn't expect a second pregnancy to produce twice as much fear.

There's been no fear left behind.

You can blame the hormones: I'm a bit of a crazy lady now. Every single time I set foot in the bathroom, I worry that I'll see red on the toilet paper, and I Google more than any pregnant woman should ever be allowed.

While reading in bed one night—our recent miscarriage still fresh in my mind—learning the statistics about possible pregnancy loss sends me into a complete panic. I convince myself that doom and gloom are destined to be ours again. As I fight to catch my breath through uncontrollable tears, my loving and kind husband starts to pray. He prays for our child, he prays for my body, and he just asks for God's hand in it all. And when my tears finally stop flowing, he hugs me and says, "I just care about your heart."

I mean, you can't make this stuff up.

I wish I could say that from that prayer on, I remain calm and enjoy the beautiful gift of carrying our child.

But we all know that's not true.

•••••••••••

A few months later, we decide to squeeze in one last international jaunt to celebrate our love of travel before we'll be landlocked for the foreseeable future by the arrival of the baby. We find a great deal on Southwest flights, and a cool boutique hotel with a rooftop pool, and we pack our bags for Puerto Rico with the expectation of six days in the sun.

If I have to be enormous, I might as well be tan.

I'm about 25 weeks pregnant, and I boldly strut around the resort in a two-piece bathing suit—the last time I'll confidently bare my midriff for quite some time. We eat decadent meals and enjoy some quiet R&R, just the two of us. I read a few great books—mainly romance novels—and sip yummy mocktails with my husband. That is, until a nasty stomach bug gets ahold of me and puts an unwelcome twist on our vacation. A quick call to the midwives to get proper sign-off on some over-the-counter remedies ends with something new to freak out about: Zika, a virus that causes severe brain defects in unborn infants, has just been announced as a major concern in the region in which we're staying.

And I already have three mosquito bites.

As the news of this terrible illness and the harm it's inflicting on fetuses spreads like wildfire across US news outlets, we're holed up in our hotel room frantically searching for return flights to Chicago in hopes of avoiding additional exposure.

My anxiety—briefly tempered by our healthy 20-week ultrasound—is back in full force, and the more I learn about the horrible reality of *microcephaly*, the more I convince myself that our child will suffer this condition.

Oh, how I wish we could take back this vacation. No tan is worth this panic.

And let's be honest, I barely tan anyway.

When we arrive back in the States, blood tests are drawn and bi-weekly ultrasounds are given. And when I walk into the midwives' office every two weeks, my stomach is in knots as I wait for a healthy report. Each time the ultrasound technician places that wand on my abdomen, I hold my breath until she tells me his head is growing at a normal rate.

It's easy to wish you hadn't allowed fear to steal joy when you've safely arrived on the other side of your prayers, but while you're living through the unknown in between, surrendering to the scary seems unavoidable.

At least, it always has for me.

Winter

The Magician

I'm still not sure where Mom found the old refrigerator boxes for my fifth birthday party, but these huge cardboard canvases were transformed into lions, giraffes, and elephants—each painted with more detail than the last. They lined the wood-paneled walls of our darkened basement, and green paper streamers hung proudly beside them. A dusty old boom box sat on the bar counter, piping in jungle noises to create an atmosphere perfect for a safari.

There were ten of us: a group of wild, excited four- and five-year-olds—each of us donning our very own safari hat and holding a flashlight. We tiptoed one by one down the stairs and were instantly immersed—hearing the monkeys, feeling the sheets of tropical "rain" come down around us. We rounded the corner and aimed our flashlights into the dimly lit room and began our trek through the rainforest, searching with eager hands for the pink-frosted animal crackers hidden among the shadows, and stowing them away in our pockets.

My mother led the way, crouching down along with us and exclaiming with delight as we explored the magical world she'd made for us. It was a birthday celebration like no other.

Could she have known that thirty years later I would still be able to recall the painted animals, practically still taste the pink-frosted animal crackers?

My Pinterest-worthy jungle birthday party was just one of countless magical memories created by my mom. My sisters and I enjoyed indoor picnic dinners and bedtime stories in the hallway and camping trips at Jellystone and summers filled with licorice ropes and nights of kick-the-can.

She was our magician, my dad her faithful assistant. Despite our family's humble beginnings, she managed to fill our childhoods with delight at every turn.

Oh, what blessed girls we were.

And with that kind of childhood—one filled with such love, intention, *joy*—do I even have permission to *consider* not providing that same experience for my own kids?

Maybe it's the fact that both Dan and I were raised by mothers who were home—Dan's childhood full of its own beautiful stories of his mother's love for her seven kids—or the fact that my past few years in sales have been nothing short of miserable for me—but my future role seems inevitable.

Assumed.

A given.

In fact, I'm not sure we've even had a formal conversation about me leaving Corporate America. We just know that I won't be working full-time after our son gets here. It's just the shared vision that's been formed for our family.

Perhaps it's been there all along.

And while I'm not sure if I'll be any good at this—I definitely can't paint jungle animals on refrigerator boxes, and I don't know where they sell pink-frosted animal crackers—I'm really liking the idea of trading in my business cards for a new job title: Mama.

My only prayer is that I can be half the magician my mom was.

Abracadabra?

Baby Medal

Someone should tell pregnant me to take a moment to really *feel* those kicks. To peek at the increasing pile of ultrasound printouts—precious profiles of our son captured in black and white—and marvel at the miracle of making a human being out of a simple act of love. To focus on the utter magnitude of creating life, rather than on the size of my fears.

Yet what do I do?

I read every blog and article I can get my hands on that recount the down-and-dirty details of labor and delivery. I read every single one, hoping to reveal it really isn't *that* bad.

(I'm sure those of you who are mothers are already laughing.)

With naïve hunger I devour tale upon tale, with two common denominators shining through: labor really flipping sucks, and delivery is really flipping beautiful. Like a marathon—although with less training runs and more carbing up—it seems pregnancy ends with this really insane event that merits both immense pride and utter astonishment that you actually made it to the finish line.

And best of all, you get a shiny medal—or baby—to prove you did it.

I will argue that at least in a marathon you're aware of the race date, have seen a course map, and don't have a husband who just ate sausage for lunch breathing in your face.

But I digress.

So, after enduring nine long months of growing a human, this impatient Mama is anxious to hear that starting gun!

Desperate for anything to get delivery underway, I waddle into a foot massage parlor for the second time in two days, with high hopes of inducing labor via pressure points in my extra swollen feet.

Thirty minutes later, I find myself wetting my pants—or so I think. A quick visit to the ladies' restroom confirms that I have not (yet) lost control of my bladder, but rather, my water just broke, and this party's about to get started.

Thank the risen cankles!

While en route home, my contractions are off to a strong start. As the pain ramps up and I blindly drive down Chicago's side streets, I call Dan, who's easily a 30-minute commute from our condo, and give him the update. Rather than run for the train, he asks if he has time to eat lunch real fast before coming home.

True story.

My uncensored response has him boarding the next train north.

Sitting on the toilet, waiting for my husband to join the fun, I snack; meanwhile, my contractions are already two minutes apart and lasting a full minute. For those of you who are blissfully ignorant to the goings-on of labor, I'm already at GO-TO-THE-HOSPITAL time and an hour hasn't even passed.

WTF?!

My labor looks nothing like what they explained at my hippie labor class!

I can't go any further without mentioning this crazy labor class. Somehow, I decided to take the most "natural" approach to childbirth, which just proves I'm a stubborn moron. In order to prepare for this self-inflicted, unnecessary torture, I signed us up for a six-week class where my very level-headed husband acted out labor, read poetry about birth, and watched *very* graphic birthing videos that caused me to cry in fear—all in the name of forgoing an epidural.

"Birth is both linear and nonlinear," the birth coach said.

"You've gotta be freaking kidding me," my husband swore. But bless his heart, he showed up for all eighteen hours of that clown show.

Too bad the labor lessons we learned were now proving just as worthless as he predicted.

Shortly after he arrives home, Dan pops his lunch in the microwave—I do not lie—while I don a fresh pair of pants. The midwife told us to come to the hospital, so I climb into the back seat of our SUV with an old beach towel beneath my leaking bottom. I moan in pain all the way down Lakeshore Drive while my chauffeur lovingly rubs my shin.

"Teamwork makes the dream work," they say.

"That is a load of bull," says every mother ever.

The intake room for Labor and Delivery has to be the most terrifying place on earth. One woman squats in the corner making guttural sounds you'd only hear at the zoo, and another weeps and holds onto her husband's hand. Then there's me, doubled over the check-in counter—standing on a towel with amniotic fluid streaming down my leg—all while waiting for my penny-pinching husband to get back from self-parking our car.

Did I mention they offer valet?

When I finally make it back into triage, they confirm what I sincerely hoped was true: I'm well into my labor. I'm already five cm dilated, and I ignorantly tell the nurse that I'd like to forgo any pain medication.

Thanks a lot, natural birthing class.

As you can imagine, this is where things take an ugly turn. I immediately feel like I'm going to black out, die, and poop myself—all at the same time. There really are no words for the pain. Let's just say those comforting, natural support measures we acted out in birthing class are instantly thrown out the window. Sorry we can't get that three hundred dollars or eighteen hours of our lives back, sweetheart. But at least we didn't waste any money on the valet parking!

And then...

Praise the risen Lord, I make it to the toilet in time to violently relieve myself not only in front of my husband for the first (dear God, let it be the last) time in our marriage but also in front of a COMPLETE STRANGER. The sweet nurse lies to me and tells me it happens all the time and it's a sign things are progressing.

Bless her heart.

To absolutely no one's surprise, I immediately tell her I'd like to order that epidural, and that I am the dumbest person I know.

The next hour while I wait for that blessed needle is a complete blur of passing out, throwing up, and finally, sweet, sweet relief. When the baby-faced anesthesiologist enters my room, I may or may not scream, "Are you an intern?!"

"I assure you, ma'am, I am not," he says.

"I'm so sorry. Please proceed."

As a friend and fellow mother once told me, an epidural is like the tears of angels. Boy, was she right.

This is when my sister, Ames, shows up and gives Dan a chance to get more food. I'm not kidding. The man needs his sustenance. We settle in to watch a nice prison reality TV show in my room—until I suddenly and violently vomit that red Gatorade I insisted on chugging on the car ride over.

I guess I'll never know the ending of that episode of *60 Days In*.

As a result of my epic purging, the nurse checks me, and after a mere forty-five minutes with that epidural, I'm at ten cm and it's pushing time. Thankfully my hubby ate quickly.

My midwife experience is wonderful; I love having a cheerleader with me through my whole delivery experience at the hospital. I'm one of those people who really needs continuous verbal affirmation—just ask my saint of a husband or my book editor—so it's huge to have someone telling me that I'm doing it right and everything is going the way it's supposed to be going.

Unfortunately, I learn that your ability to back squat does not translate into efficiency at pushing a baby out. This business is HARD. When I ask the midwife how many sets of these pushes I have left—thank you CrossFit—she smiles kindly and says she'd put her money on me being able to do it in less than ten.

And together, the three of us get that baby out of me in seven.

And just like that, there he is.

My Micah King.

All 8 pounds and 11 ounces of his smushy, cone-headed self. He screams his way into the world while tears stream down my face. (Which is really a metaphor for how we spend most of his first year of life, but I hesitate to ruin this beautiful moment with those details.)

Delivering a child is shocking in its beauty. *Shocking.*

I had no idea how amazing it would be to become a mother. To see a person—a living soul—take his first breath is mind-blowing. To know that this very soul was woven by your two hearts, sewn by the hands of the Father, and formed inside your body, is completely earth-shattering.

And to be given the honor of writing the very first page of my son's story?

There are no words.

There is only love—love in its deepest, purest form. Love that transforms your soul forever. Love that will never leave you. Love that lives, becomes.

So after 9 months of pregnancy, 400 pints of ice cream, 2 foot massages, 1 toilet snack, 1 *very* public display of diarrhea, 2 lunches for my husband, 1 epidural, and only 6 hours of labor, we have one beautiful baby boy.

And I am starving.

Made for Three

Sweaty brow, aching limbs.
A healthy cry.
Relief so deep.
Painful parts. Why so painful?
A perfect tiny person.
Joy. Immeasurable love.
Mesh underwear. Adult diaper. Bucket of pain meds.
Smallest fingers. Littlest toes.
Exhausted. Delirious.
Baby screaming, leaking boobs.
A latch. A wince. An exhale.
Never letting go.
Heart bursting. Body bleeding.
Expert nurses. Eager Dad.
Remember these moments.
Pull the car around. Are you sure he's okay?
Climb in the back seat. A yelp and a yawn.
Can't stop staring.
So much traffic. Stop and go.
Look at all the people. Once a baby.
Mind blown.
Grab the bags. And the baby.
Hold the elevator. Catch his eyes.
Smile. Nervous laugh.
Ushered in with excitement.
Can't wait for cold cuts. Finally, a glass of wine.
So much pride.
Hot shower. Fresh clothes.
Sitting gingerly.

Still in awe.
Everything here is the same.
But feels so different.
This home was made for three.
A feeding.
A fresh diaper.
Fast asleep.
Repeat.
Repeat.
Repeat.
Head on pillow.
Grateful for Grandma.
Fast asleep.
Piercing cry.
Here we go. You got this.
Mama.
A dark nursery and a lullaby.
First moments alone together.
Gentle prayers. Quiet tears.
And the gift becomes true.
You are a mother. And he is yours.
Forever.

Fourth Trimester

This Is Motherhood

It's 2 AM and I want a divorce.

Except that wouldn't be a great idea. After all, if being a mom is hard, the life of a single mom would only be that much harder. Who would bring me a glass of water or make a quick dinner while I pump? Who would empty the Diaper Genie??

That's right. Better to stick it out. Stay together. Hold the vow. Avoid the diaper trash.

But man, this little one is not what I expected. Motherhood isn't what I expected. Wasn't it supposed to be magical? I imagined all of the cuddles and none of the struggles. I imagined all of the cute family pictures and none of the up-all-night. I imagined all of the laughter and none of the crying.

No, screaming. It's more like screaming, isn't it?

Silly me.

Those other women have it so much more together. Their children must not cry all night. Or poop. It's probably formula. Should we switch to formula? Why won't he take a pacifier? Or stay in a swaddle? Thank God for that damn swing. It's the most beautiful eyesore I've ever seen.

Seriously, will my house ever look nice again? Or clean?

So.

Much.

Stuff.

Maybe in five years. No, make that seven. He can't be an only child. Or can he? But the parents of an only child must be so rested. And have so much more money in savings. And they must take vacations.

Oh, vacations. How I miss you.

Once upon a time, we traveled through Europe for over four months. That was such a long time ago. Or was it? I guess two years isn't that long ago, but it feels like a lifetime. Now we'd have to get a baby passport. Or a live-in mother-in-law. Passport is easier. I wonder how they take their little mug shots? Good thing we live next to a pharmacy photo center. Remind me to email the husband about registering for a baby passport. And to talk to his mother about babysitting soon.

Babysitters. I never thought these city limits would be so limiting. We are on an island. An urban island flooded with traffic and bad parking and no help.

God, I miss my mom.

I'm tired. Bone tired. How did my mom do it with two babes only a year apart? And bless her, my mother-in-law with *seven* kids? I swear they didn't tell me about this level of exhaustion. My emotions are barely being kept under the surface and I legitimately feel like a crazy person. Did I already tell you that?

Well, you already knew that.

There is a magical little person in my lap, but he's here all the time. My lap is his favorite place. Why wouldn't it be? It's next door to his first home. We prayed for him. I longed for him. Yet I resent his utter dependence on me. And my husband's inability to swoop in and help.

Or to read my mind. Can't he see I have to pee? Or these dark circles? If only he had boobs. But not man boobs.

Gross. Why is this job so gross?

Poop, puke, boogers. Did you know you have to suck the boogers out of their little noses? While they scream bloody murder, of course.

But then they can breathe.

And finally, so can you.

And you start to find yourself again.

You find a magical sleep sack that he feels so secure in. You drench him in essential oils that help him sleep a bit longer. Your body adjusts to the sleep deprivation—it no longer feels like some kind of sadistic torture ritual. You start to remember which day of the week it is.

Speaking of deprivation, you try to lose those last few pounds of baby weight. It's not a perfect battle but you start to feel more like yourself. You fit back into your skinny yoga pants. And you buy an expensive nursing bra so you have real support in your life again. It even has a little lace. You almost feel sexy again.

Almost.

And you go get your hair highlighted at the nice salon, and for the first time in your life you actually relish how long it takes to put in all those foils. And they serve good coffee. And, oh my goodness, it's still hot. Bliss with bleach.

And your baby is old enough for childcare at the gym! A new gym of course. No more CrossFit, but weightlifting and tennis will do. And there's free parking. You sneak your old SUV into the space between a Tesla and a minivan, and you wonder for the first time in your life why anyone would invest in a luxury vehicle when they could instead have easy access to the car seats, extra storage, and self-sliding doors?

And you shake your head at your new normal.

You shake your head when his blow-out happens right as you walk out the gym door, but this time, you don't tear up. This time you laugh at your little stinker, and cherish his sweet giggle while you tickle him during his diaper change. Oh, the progress in that!

Thank God for the simple reminders to slow down.

Then you sleep-train over a bottle of wine—and shed more tears than the baby—on the back porch at sunset. You celebrate by having a real conversation with your husband for the first time in ages. And you remember that he was a good choice.

He was always a good choice. Why did I hate him again?

He encourages your tired mama heart in all the right ways. He says he's proud of you and that you're a good mom, even though you know you're not who you thought you would be in this role.

In some ways you're so much more. You are your child's perfect safe place. You instinctively know the definition of each cry, and you always wake up before he does. Even on those rare occasions when he isn't crying. You've never given more of yourself to anyone in your entire life.

But in some ways you are so much less. You lose your patience with an infant. And your husband. And yourself. You forget your footing is secure even as the waves crash into you.

But you learn to take bigger breaths and dig in those heels. His mercies are new each morning.

Thank.

You.

Sweet.

Jesus.

You slowly find your tribe of mamas who text you back at 3 AM to tell you how to survive teething and how to get your child to take a freaking bottle. And they don't care if all you talk about is your baby's sleep patterns, and they offer tested advice to help get through the day. The week. The year.

And they remind you that in order to give so much of yourself, you have to refuel. And you start to create space for yourself again. Little bits of space. And finally, some order comes back into your life.

And you take a deep breath of gratitude for all that has been entrusted to you. For every sweet moment with this sweet babe of yours, the closest thing you'll get to a miracle this side of Heaven.

And then there's the gut-wrenching irony of watching that little miracle, that literal piece of your soul, living out in a world that doesn't promise it will be kind to him.

And it terrifies you.

I'm glad you don't know about the rough patches ahead. Or the sweet ones. Life is so gloriously precious and utterly scary, isn't it?

They say it's all worth it. The best job on earth. But I think that's a cop-out. Of course becoming a mother has been more than worth it, but as far as the daily job goes, let's be honest, it kind of sucks. Sometimes I feel oh-so-overqualified, but other days, I consider tendering my resignation out of the sheer weight of the role.

Well excuse me, I have to go pump. I always have to go pump. Or nurse. Or both. Yeah, figure out them nipples.

I mean apples.

Well, I guess this is motherhood. And I thank God for it.

Summer

Tribe and True

*I*t's been way too long since I've gotten together with my best friends. The baby's debut is partly to blame, but the girls have also all been caught up with the heavy travel demands of their successful careers—a brutal combination in the scheduling department. Which is how we ended up penciling in some face time for a weeknight smack dab in the middle of Micah's bedtime routine.

Since my babe is still attached to the boob, I'm forced to roll in thirty minutes late with a store-bought appetizer in hand. They're already a few glasses in, and it's evident by the abrupt halt in conversation that I'm interrupting a lively discussion.

"Oh, Lyss. Perfect timing! Since you were late, we already had the chance to get our job updates out of the way, so you don't have to be bored through them."

"Oh, okay."

And my heart sinks with the realization that they no longer consider me someone worth including in their discussion of professional endeavors. I guess my new title of "stay-at-home mother" erases that college degree I earned and that enormous sales territory I built over the past few years. Apparently my work experience is no longer relevant.

And perhaps, neither am I.

In an effort to disguise my disappointment, I suck down way too much wine and plaster a smile on my face. We carry on about our marriages and the latest dating apps, I share the more exciting news updates from Micah's little life—rolling over, solid foods, sleep training—and we gossip about our old college friends' Facebook pictures.

For someone who usually has another person constantly attached to her body, I feel completely alone.

• • • • • • • • • • •

When breastfeeding in front of a new friend who's also a nursing mom, it's always one of those questions of who's going to ditch their cover first. After her girls are out, I gain the confidence to throw caution—and my nipples—to the wind as well.

There's something about baring your breasts in front of someone that immediately encourages baring your soul.

This is how Sarah becomes my lifeline in these early months of parenting. With our boys only a few weeks apart and both of us embarking on the new career journey of raising our children at home on our own, it doesn't take long before we're sharing more than just our bra size.

Her little guy rivals mine in his lack of desire to sleep. Her husband struggles to understand the demands of her days in light of the weight of his own. She worries about the financial pressure of her choice to stay at home. She gives all of herself at all hours and at all costs.

And she often finds herself up in the middle of the night in need of an encouraging friend. So do I.

Basically, Sarah's life looks a whole lot like mine. And I breathe a sigh of relief.

I finally feel a little less alone.

• • • • • • • • • • •

I may have had to incorporate a combination of lying flat on my back, carefully lunging, and engaging my copyrighted booty-shimmying-and-tugging combination, but my favorite pre-pregnancy jeans are on my body. They finally FIT!

It's only taken six months.

And I'll be damned, I'm going to shout it from the rooftops. Which is how I end up shooting my very first selfie while standing in front of my hall mirror and sending it to my closest girlfriends.

Group text to my childless besties:

#prepregnancyjeans {all the praise hands emojis}

First response:

Big day at Mariano's (the local grocery store) *today, Lyss?*

I'll admit that I can usually be seen in my infamous athleisure getup, but seriously? Wearing denim is not that noteworthy. Plus who would be dumb enough to bother putting on jeans for the grocery store? Obviously I'm going to my physical therapy appointment—easily my best dressed morning each week (since a severe tear mutilated my lady parts when I delivered an enormous child).

My text back:

Nope just going to get that good old vag PT. Something about having a stranger digging around in there makes a girl want to look nice.

But even my sarcasm can't hide my hurt. My stay-at-home life has been misconstrued as dressing up for grocery runs.

Do I no longer fit into more than just my jeans?

••••••••••••

The first thing I notice about Lauren is her adorable accent. Well, that and her really flat stomach and sad face.

She recently arrived in Chicago via Kentucky, and today she shuffles in late—city traffic!—with her two gorgeous blonde boys in tow. She hustles them down to the babysitter and sits across from me at our very first church-led Moms group.

We only last a few weeks in the group. Far too much work for a Monday morning.

But when Lauren emails me with some tried-and-true natural

remedies for Micah's first serious cold, I invite the three of them to meet the two of us for cinnamon rolls.

As we start that awkward process of attempting to get to know another adult, all the while wrangling babies and toddlers (no conversation free of interruption or poop), we learn that maybe we both really need each other. And that this is a friendship worth the effort.

When we stand side-by-side in a park later that summer and I drop my first F-bomb in her presence—and she a pastor's wife to boot—she replies, "Oh, thank God."

And just like that, I also *swear* we'll be forever friends.

She teaches me how to heal a diaper rash, and I help her figure out public transportation. She assures me everything I'm feeling about motherhood is totally normal, and I assure her everything about living in a new city will get easier. She promises me I'm a good mama, and I promise her Chicago will become home.

And together, we build each other up in all the ways we need during these tough months of transition.

There Is A Christmas Tree

Nightmares

S ame stage, different day.

It's an ugly time in the middle of the night and the baby's crying. Again.

Our little family is fresh off a five-day stomach plague that had us miserable on all ends, if you know what I mean. We're overtired, cranky and desperate for a good night's sleep. And as a breastfeeding mama who's been on solo nighttime duty for the duration of my nine-month-old's life, I'm especially miserable. Daddy helps in the early mornings, but we have a baby who knows what he wants, has yet to master self-soothing, and makes his preferences known to us (and every neighbor on our floor) if Dad tries to save Mom some REM cycles.

We're in a vicious and tired cycle, and we're ripe for conflict.

We've tried every version of sleep training out there, and we still haven't kicked Micah's night-waking habit. Now, after I've let him "work through it" for close to a half hour, I'm half losing it. For whatever reason, whenever my baby cries, I get triggered. I blame biology—our milk lets down in response to their noisemaking, for heaven's sake. But rather than getting angry at the baby, or relenting to soothe him in spite of our sleep training, I lash out, white hot, against the closest victim: my *sound-asleep, softly-snoring* husband.

You heard that I've been letting the baby "work through it" for thirty minutes, right? Yes. My husband doesn't seem to suffer from my son's inability to sleep through the night.

Lucky him. Martyr me.

So you get the picture. I'm ready for an outburst, and Dan is going to hear it from me. That is, if he ever wakes up. Enter my loud, passive-aggressive muttering to "myself," and he finally rolls over and asks the world's most annoying question ever: "How long has he been going for?"

My husband doesn't stand a chance after this. I self-righteously berate him about my feeling completely alone in parenting, how mad I am that he's never read any of the sleep books, and how I'm absolutely sick of having to do every. Single. Night. Alone.

I storm out, grab my wailing child, throw him on the boob and stew in my anger for twenty minutes. I'm telling you, there are some *ugly* thoughts running through my head tonight.

But I'm guessing you can see who the ugly one is in this situation.

To make matters worse, as soon as I've finally lulled Micah into a (hopefully) deep and lasting slumber, I wake my sleeping husband to tell him the thoughts I've so perfectly crafted during my umpteen-millionth night-nursing session, and lodge a full-on attack that ends with my husband sleeping on the couch—his first ever conflict-driven overnight stay in our family room.

We've reached a crossroads marked by my accusations and his inability to read my mind. We can no longer pretend things will magically just get better by morning. Something needs to change, and it's staring at me in the mirror.

Later, my transgressions are fully illuminated in the darkness of my now-lonely room. I approach my banished husband with remorse and tears of shame and tell him I can't sleep without him. As he crawls back into bed, we both know that while this feels better than going to bed angry and apart, we'll need to do a lot more to reduce the distance between us than just make room in our bed.

And we both need that sweet child to sleep.

When I try to tackle these big issues late at night—or in this case, the flipping middle of the night—my husband tends to just quietly listen rather than fanning the flame. Probably because he's always been oh-so-wise. However, this often backfires and we end up worse for wear. Knowing this too-familiar pattern, you'd think I'd save my concerns for the breakfast table when everyone's at their best—or at least when my audience is. But no, I like to show off my maturity and let things sort of erupt out of me in a messy jumbled outpouring of emotion. Let's just say, in the conflict resolution class, I'm getting a solid failing grade.

Please tell me I'm not the only one.

As I write this, I'm listening to a playlist that my sweet husband spontaneously made for me that he labeled "LTD" for music of our Life To Date. One of our favorites, Ben Rector's "White Dress," repeats, "I never knew that I could love someone the way that I love you. I never knew, I never knew." But the part that has always stood out to me is when he repeats back, "I never knew that you could love someone like me. I never knew, I never knew."

The bigger shock isn't how much we could love another human being. It's how anyone could ever love us back that much. That's scarier. After all, we know the fullness of our ugliness from the inside out. Can't he see it? Doesn't Dan see my selfishness? Doesn't he know I'm a finger-pointer?

Doesn't he know better than to be with a woman who makes nightmares in the middle of the night?

Oh, but that's the secret to love. In its purest form, love is being fully known and fully accepted. Even with the nightmares. And I can definitely take ownership of a few of those throughout our story.

And per usual, it always goes back to the Gospel, doesn't it? Failure and sin are met with grace and unexplainable love. What I'm striving for in my marriage relationship is to become the gospel to my husband: meeting him with grace and love when he fails to be my current—i.e. ever-changing—version of perfect. Because I really do love that man. Even when my failure to love him well is what we see.

In this difficult season for the two of us—*ahem,* new parents— I've had to seek time alone with the Lord more than ever before. For the record, this usually happens while I'm listening to some heavenly music and sweating at the gym. Did I mention my gym has free childcare? Hey, I'm no perfect picture of worship.

Yet He always meets me—no matter the method I use to try to find Him.

So as I surrender my mess in these moments, nightmares and all, God is slowly showing me that if I want my marriage to have a fighting chance in this broken, broken world, I need to learn to fight well. And that's not just with Dan. That's in my messy brain. My messy heart. My messy soul. It shows in how I'm praying, how I'm spending my time, and who I'm surrounding myself with.

All of it.

There is no love story—or any story for that matter—that doesn't have some conflict. What counts is what I bring to the conflict. And that starts with what's on the inside.

My brain.

My heart.

My soul.

Admittedly, they're all just a bit ugly right now.

But there's only one place I can count on going for a good cleanup: Before the throne of the One whose love is boundless.

Why does it always take me so long to get there?

Rather than be conflict-provoking, as I can often be, or conflict-avoidant, like my better half, we need to allow our conflict to become a chance to fight *for each other* instead. We've been given a chance to build something whole and tangled and beautiful, and it's worth every effort. Rather than let our conflict break us apart, I'm asking God to redeem it and make us better together than we are alone.

And when all else fails, my husband reminds me that we can do hard things. We can turn this marriage—and ourselves—inside out and find the beauty. We always have a fighting chance. So I will try to fight well. I choose to fight for my marriage instead of fighting with my husband.

And I may turn up the volume button on the baby monitor.

The Climb We Fall, Revisited

I walked into motherhood the way most girls pledge a sorority: with a lot of joy and pride for being chosen to wear the badge of honor, but ignorant to the hazing that was about to follow. Imagining all the cute new songs and none of the throwing up into garbage cans while surrounded by fraternity brothers.

The parallels here are plentiful.

It's embarrassing to admit that I have not adjusted well to becoming a mom. I'm convinced that I've cried more in the last year than in the ten years leading up to it combined. And I promise you, sleep deprivation is an actual form of torture. A year into exclusively breastfeeding a total mama's boy, and I don't remember the last time I felt like myself. And on top of that, Mom Brain is real, folks. Trust me, basically all the time you really do feel like a crazy person who can never find her keys.

On the cusp of a mental breakdown caused by my sleep-defying baby and the fact that I'm an emotionally unprepared mother, I've started going to therapy again. My therapist (read: paid best friend) finally put my version of the truth of motherhood into words: *"It's okay if becoming a mother was both the best and worst thing to ever happen to you."*

Preach, sister.

But the hardest part of this mountain of motherhood that I'm climbing?

It seems like all the other moms have molehills. Or they must have been better trained and equipped to make the trek; they must have splurged on a Sherpa! There's nothing like a bit of comparison— so easily fostered in our social media age—to make you feel like absolute garbage and a complete failure all rolled into one.

"*Give up,*" that dark voice says.

"*You're not good at this,*" my fragile heart believes.

And the tears stream again.

Maybe some women have plenty of people to carry their bags, or balanced hormones, or sleeping babies. I have none of these things. Or maybe they feel wholly and utterly fulfilled in the way I thought I was supposed to feel. I'm well aware that my mountain could be bigger (said paid best friend had two *severely* colicky babies back-to-back), steeper (could you imagine having multiples?), or worse, not exist at all.

And now enter the guilt about not feeling grateful enough for my motherhood.

I swear, the lies are steeper than the climb itself.

But just like that trip to Peru so many years ago, even though I'm loving the views and the memory-making, there are times where I hate and resent the act of getting here. For me, it feels like it's been raining every darn day of this trip!

I'm not the only one, right?

So after some important self-reflection—and the affirmation of a professional who verbalized the dichotomy of my experience in becoming a mom—I am here to tell you that you can love your kids and hate some parts of raising them.

And just like Machu Picchu, I'll be glad I took so many damn pictures and will remember this ascent as a turning point in my life. But let me tell you, sometimes I wish I'd just chosen an all-inclusive beach vacation instead.

Wouldn't that have been easier?

Fewer pictures and milestones—definitely less baby food and diapers—but there would be the promise of more rest and perhaps a tan.

....

And just like that, I'm back on that godforsaken mountainside. Great. The rain has been replaced with a cloudless sky, the afternoon sun is beating down on me, and I am so, so thirsty. I'm always so thirsty! Where did I leave my water bottle again? Is Dan ever going to come back?

My muscles ache and I feel like I have nothing left. I claw away at the mountainside, but I still feel the earth move beneath me, even without gaining any ground. I look up and can't see the top. Hopelessness closes in, and I struggle to catch my breath. Minutes, hours, years pass, and the fear suffocates me. I see nothing but black.

This is where I'm going to die. And for once, I don't even care.

In a desperate surrender, I stop and fall against the cold, damp earth. After a few moments, I roll onto my back, dig in my feet, open my eyes, and take in the view from the side of the mountain. Somehow, by God's grace, this time I don't slide down.

I feel safe. Could I be safe?

Why didn't I realize earlier that I could take a break? I just needed to stop and lean.

Green treetops and rolling hills fan out below me. The sunshine warms my cheeks; the orange and pink hues of an incredible sunset take my breath away. I see an eagle soaring in the distance and suddenly hear the soft rush of water from a nearby stream. Like a miracle, it's close enough that I'm able to scoot over, reach in, and scoop up a drink of water.

Was that here before?

I fall back and close my eyes. My entire body begins to relax. I inhale the fresh, warm air and exhale with a soft sob.

I can finally breathe.

It's in that exact moment that a soft whisper dances in the wind: "Be still, child. I am here. I was always here," it says.

And this time, in the middle of a mountainside sunset, I lean back and fall asleep, knowing that I am not alone.

PART TWO: LETTING GO

Summer

Healing Broken Souls

We have a kid who doesn't sleep, a neighbor in desperate need of a more subtle alarm clock, and an interior condo bedroom with lofted walls (a feature that seemed trendy to us as newlyweds, but is torture to new parents). So, right around Micah's first birthday, in reckless abandon of our budget, Dan and I begin touring larger living spaces in the city in a last-ditch attempt to reclaim our sleep and, hopefully, our sanity.

With my mother's "no shoe" rule forever ingrained in my mind, I find myself exploring a three-story townhouse *sans* shoes. That is, until my slippery athletic socks fail me on a steep carpeted staircase. One desperate grasp to a railing saves my boys from similar demise—Dan's carrying Micah in front of me—but it lands me with a need for shoulder surgery.

Great.

It's already been a tricky and sleepless year, rife with exhaustion for both of us and a nice bout of recent postpartum depression for me—leaving me weepy, distant, and just plain mean more days than not. And even though we're hopeful that our lives—and, please Jesus, our sleep—will improve since we did end up moving into a bigger townhouse, we now have the challenge of getting through an unexpected surgery to ruin what should have been a carefree summer of enjoying our first private backyard in ten years of living in Chicago.

And to make matters worse, I come out on the other side of my procedure to learn that they had to repair my labrum, rotator cuff, and biceps—more work than anticipated and subsequently a longer recovery.

Despite stocking up on ice and prepping freezer meals, nothing can prepare this stay-at-home mother for just how awful it will be to become so dependent on everyone. To keep our family from falling apart, my mom graciously moves into our new guest bedroom and Dan takes a sabbatical from work. Between the two of them, they care for Micah and me twenty-four hours a day.

Not only am I chained to a La-Z-Boy® recliner on loan from my in-laws, but my pain and effort to simply get through the day is unimaginable. Narcotics and Netflix become my lifelines. Worst of all, my son can't understand why "Mama" can't be "Mama." Through tears he'll reach for me, and someone else has to pick him up instead. It will take two months before I can properly hug my son, and four months before I can pick him up with both hands.

Talk about gut-wrenching.

Praise God, my sweet boy is so well loved in spite of my physical limitations, but I'll be honest, the first time he pushes me away to reach for his Daddy after scraping his knees, I can't stop the tears from pouring out of me. I'm brokenhearted. Thanks to surgery, my only job has been stolen from me, and my sense of purpose has gone with it.

Before long, I fall into a depression darker than anything I've ever experienced.

The only way to describe my existence that summer is to say that my world becomes blanketed with a loneliness and pain—both physical and emotional—that I didn't know was possible. I don't have the energy to get up in the morning, and often I give in and stay in bed (or in my case, chair). Simple tasks take incredible effort. I look at a dirty plate and the sheer thought of carrying it to the dishwasher seems an impossible endeavor. More days than not, I find myself sobbing in that damn recliner.

As I sink deeper into my depression, the lies become louder. They tell me I'm a bad mother and an even worse wife, and my family would be better off without me. All I see is my worthlessness. I have nothing to offer this world. I'm a burden. I have no purpose.

For the first time in my life, I consider how easy it would be to step off the "El" platform as the Red Line is zipping down the tracks.

I'm broken.

Depression is from Satan himself—the one who comes to steal, kill, and destroy. And boy, oh boy, that he does.

But thank God for professionals and saintly, supportive spouses.

My counselor has said that when one person in a family is suffering from depression, so is the whole household. Right now, there are no corners of my family's lives that aren't impacted by my new state of darkness. My selfless husband—biting back all complaints for the sake of love (and probably for fear of backlash)—tirelessly changes every diaper and washes every one of my dirty dishes. He fetches me ice and Oxy and rubs the menacing knots in my shoulder blades each night. He may lack the words to heal me—and the skills to tie a proper ponytail—but he never lets go of my hand. He sits next to me as I cry and allows me space to grieve the incredible sense of loss that only I can feel. He sacrifices work, friends, and sleep, continually battling his own fears regarding this new version of his wife. Micah adapts to life at daycare and one-armed side hugs, and my boys develop a beautiful closeness that brings my heart both sweet comfort and deep envy all at the same time.

But while they adjust, I retreat. Depression wants no audience.

And yet.

God sends me His angels in the form of my sisters—a brave few friends bold enough to seek me out as I bury my head in the sand. If there is one sure cure for the devil's lies when you can't hear God's voice, it's a truth-bearing community telling you that you are not alone, not broken, and that hope hasn't left you.

My friend, Ellen, shares that during her own depression she felt like she was being held underwater. Lauren's experience caused her to have no concrete memories for several months of her life while she was raising two young boys in a new city. Katie's atypical depression actually brought her to a psychotic break in her early twenties. Emma relied on meds to help her get through a rough college experience. And Sara finally got help after she realized that she hadn't bathed for a whole week, her co-workers' loving concern finally providing the encouragement she needed to seek professional help.

I swear, the power of hearing *"You are not alone."* is from Jesus Himself.

And with that knowledge, little by little, I'm pulled towards the light. Suddenly I can see my Savior's arms reaching down towards me.

And His arms look like my husband's, holding me while I cry. His eyes see that I just need my mom; and with His foresight, she's with us four times that summer, despite living eighteen hundred miles away. His hands offer me a glass of wine/La Croix/coffee to share with those dear friends who were delivered from their own bouts of depression and chose to be vulnerable with me to proclaim hope after sorrow—and sometimes medication.

His love brings me back to my counselor's office with a heart that's finally willing to consider a prescription to help set my brain back in balance. His grace brings me to a physical therapist who fervently believes in my athletic future and cheers me on with every small rehab victory. And finally, His voice whispers to me in the dark and says, "Write."

"Alyssa, just write."

And as I begin to pour myself out before the screen, I can feel myself being pulled upwards.

•••••••••••

Sometimes deliverance is a process. Although I'm desperate for a quick fix, instead, the Lord is healing my broken soul and body with slow, deliberate care. At times it isn't clear if I'm going to make it, but slowly—*ever so slowly*—I feel the sunshine on my face and the breeze in my hair—which I can finally put in a ponytail with my own two hands! And one afternoon, as I'm walking down an industrial city street—in the most unlikely of places—I'm overtaken by the scent of a burning wood fire, my all-time favorite reminder of childhood, summer, and God's love for us. And in my spirit, I know this moment is just for me.

I sense the Spirit's presence for the first time in months.

Just like that, I notice all of Micah's new words and see his baby cheeks thinning out. I marvel at his dexterity at climbing slides, and I enjoy watching his brain come alive. And I joyfully name and mimic each animal he points out in his books.

Every.

Single.

Time.

And I finally feel Dan's love for me—in his sacrifice.

Slowly, and then suddenly, I become a part of my life again. My soul has been awakened.

My dear friend (in the sense that we've spent a lot of time together, but not in the sense that we've ever met) Kari Jobe, carries me through these hard summer months with her soul-lifting gift of writing songs that allow me to feel the fullness of my pain but hiding truth among the notes. Her voice becomes a healing salve to my wounded spirit, her lyrics a beacon of hope promising my broken soul can find wholeness again.

Today I am grateful for the four scars that now circle my shoulder, their presence a permanent reminder, tattooed on my body, of this season of brokenness and of His healing. For He has carefully healed what was broken in me—both physically and in spirit. And just like my Savior's, those scars will be my lifelong reminder of God's perfect love for me.

For, each step of the way, He was healing my broken soul. I may have fallen further than ever before, but I was never out of His reach.

Reflecting on my season of depression and anxiety, I'm reminded of the Red Sea and the Israelites who walked through it. The Jewish people were running for their lives—enormous walls of water standing on either side of them, threatening to come crashing down at any moment—with a leader they barely knew at their head, and the Egyptian army on their tail.

Can you even imagine?

They were literally walking through a miracle—one that displayed God's immeasurable power and His saving grace all at the same time—and all they had was their faith to spur them on.

Do you think they were scared? Or were they overwhelmed with the joy of the saving journey unrolling before them?

I wonder, did one of them stop to pick up a stone from the dry sea floor? Did he carry it in his hand until he reached the other side? Clutching a small memento in his palm to remind him of the day the Lord delivered him from the hands of his enemies, proof that He really was the God of miracles—one who could part a sea and save His people. Did he cling to that physical reminder of that incredible rescue mission for the next forty years? So that, as he choked down manna and wandered the wilderness—as his hope in God's promises waned and the years ticked by—he could cling to that rock as testament to the goodness of his God?

I sure hope so.

Dan likes to tell me that the best way to build our trust in the Lord's goodness is to build a faith wall—one that's built with stones shaped by God's promises and bricks formed by our answered prayers. He tells me that in the moments where the power of God is at work in our lives and we're able to notice the floors of our own Red Seas—the times where His marvels are tangible and real—we should reach down and take a bit of those miracles with us. We should collect these little bits of proof that God has been with us—that He has delivered us—in our hearts forever.

We should never let them go.

And as we hold onto our personal mementos of His love, in time, our faith wall will become taller, stronger, more secure. It will become an impenetrable fortress of trust. So that when the water comes crashing down and our circumstances force us to question His faithfulness—or just His existence at all—our faith will be strong enough to stand against our fear, our darkness.

So, will I remember to pick up my stone from this deliverance? Will I lay this brick on top of my answered prayer to be brought out of my depression? Will I set it next to the stone that was a desire to heal from my shoulder injury? Will it sit upon the rock of my dream to be a part of my life again?

And with these layers, will my faith wall become stronger than my fears?

I sure hope so.

July

Just Call Me Mom (Maybe)

I keep seeing these pregnant women at the park. Their hair is styled, their baby bumps look like perky little basketballs under their adorable on-trend maternity blouses, and their well-behaved toddlers smile as they gracefully glide feet-first down the slide.

I swear, they even look well-rested.

Meanwhile, I haven't showered since Tuesday and I'm wearing my go-to mom uniform of Lululemon crops and a Cubs hat to hide my greasy hair. To make matters worse, I just realized I'm in desperate need of a pedicure—my chipped big toenail defies my attempt to look put together with every step. Oh, and after tumbling head-first down the tornado slide, Micah steals some kid's sidewalk chalk and proceeds to shove it into his mouth and run away. After chasing him down and peeling it from between his teeth, I get to experience his new affinity for throwing himself on the ground in a full-body tantrum while he defiantly smears his blue-chalked hands all over my aforementioned black crop pants.

This is my life.

Bribing him with the promise of a delicious (read: store-bought, definitely processed, but certifiably organic) snack when we get home, I finally calm him down, and I hand the stolen goods back to our well-dressed (and, you guessed it, pregnant!) neighbor. I apologize for my runaway thief and make an awkward joke about stifling the passions of a true artist.

The only thing graceful about the DeRose family is our exit.

After I wrangle Micah back into his push-car for the short tree-lined walk to our Roscoe Village row home, I can't shake the feeling that I'm so far from being one of those women—both in dress and in desire to have another child. How is it that all these people around us are happily growing their families, having multiple kids in quick succession? How come that very idea makes both Dan and me look at each other in terror? How come I don't seem to like large chunks of this whole motherhood gig? (Trying to manage my unruly toddler at the park in front of other put-together parents tops my list.)

Before entering the throes of parenthood, Dan and I might have claimed to want four kids. I'm not saying I don't dream of summer camping trips and backyard movie nights with a healthy-sized brood, but getting from where we are today to making memories like that seems incredibly daunting. If I'm being honest with myself, I just don't understand how everyone around me seems to be building these big beautiful families, and seemingly with such enviable grace, when we can barely keep it together with just one.

And as for grace, motherhood for this Mama has been anything but graceful so far.

•••••••••••

The next morning, I take a positive pregnancy test.

Yes, you read that correctly.

You see, I started a low dose of anti-anxiety medication this month after finally accepting that I need a little bit of Big Pharma help in managing my mental health after a shit sandwich of a summer. I saw my longtime primary care doctor and she wrote me a script and warned me to be on the lookout for some mild side effects: nausea, headaches, and dizziness.

So after a couple days of experiencing crazy vertigo, I think I'll take a quick pregnancy test to prove that it's *just* the Zoloft. And just like two years ago, I sneak into our bathroom to calm my crazy while Dan's blissfully unaware of my testing. So when a very faint second line starts to appear, I instantly take two more tests, proving three times over that I'd better go tell my husband what I'm up to. He's downstairs feeding our toddler cheesy scrambled eggs before daycare when I casually mention I have three positive pregnancy tests next to the sink upstairs.

"That is impossible," he says.

"Well is it, though?" I reply.

"Wow," is all he can muster in response.

And just like that, my feelings are hurt that he's not more excited. If only because admitting to myself that I'm not more excited would make me a bad Mom.

That afternoon I make an appointment to see my midwife and buy some prenatal vitamins so I can convince myself that I *am* indeed cut out for this again. I call my Mom and sisters and actually say out loud for the first time that we have a new family member on the way. I even dare to consider that it could be a girl—oh, the clothes!—and I immediately begin praying that this next one will be easier.

They sleep better the second time around, right?

My, oh my, what have we gotten ourselves into?

•••••••••••

The thing about being a woman is that motherhood will never be fair. Beginning on those first few pages of Scripture, we're promised that this part of our female story is going to be cursed.

"There will be pain in childbirth."

Thanks a lot, Eve.

From what I've learned while walking alongside my friends during these really big years where we start to think about the big job of having children, or perhaps our lack of desire or ability to, all of us have had the weight of that original curse upon our shoulders in one way or another—the curse transcending just the physical act of childbirth. If there's one thing I have witnessed, it's Satan's creativity in targeting us all.

Some of us can't attend a family event without every other relative asking about our dating prospects or gently hinting that we're not getting any younger, their curiosity about our singleness highlighting the very insecurities we fight daily to deny. Too many of us have felt the utter joy and subsequent overwhelming heartbreak of losing a pregnancy or adoption. Others of us have been to countless doctors' appointments trying to understand the root cause of our infertility, choosing to undergo treatment after treatment for the mere chance of carrying a biological child.

And as the months and years pass by as we wait for God to move in our hopes for motherhood, our faith often wanes with each turning of the page in the calendar.

And then there are the mothers among us: tired, flawed lovers of these little (and not-so-little) humans who happen to bring out every best and worst part of ourselves. We carry the weight of protecting their lives in spite of the fact that we actually have no control over them. We worry about their health, their hearts, and their futures, and we recognize how inadequate we are for such a huge responsibility. We fail our children and ourselves over and over and over again, and question the calling of motherhood altogether.

Some of us even regret it a little bit.

We also recognize that there are mothers among us who have had to say utterly unfair goodbyes to their life's greatest gifts. And many of those mothers, in their devastating grief, struggle to see God's goodness. Oh Lord, be near to the brokenhearted.

And still, God has promised that He is there among us all, no matter where we are in our journey. Sadly, He doesn't promise us that this life will always be pain-free, but we know He's the God of miracles. And I pray daily that He'll give me the eyes to see His miracles when my circumstances tell me they do not exist.

I choose to practice gratitude and do my best to release my fears. I ask for God to hear my heart, and I *really* try to trust that those plans of His are better than mine. And when I struggle to trust Him, I'm grateful for my sisters who walk alongside me and hold my hand—sometimes you just need another human being to be with you in those moments of doubt, don't you?

So no matter where you are in your story of motherhood and womanhood, I ask for God to be near to you. I ask for Him to be the voice that speaks louder than the liar who tells you that you don't deserve the joys of this life.

And I ask for you to be reminded that even in spite of that dang curse, there's also a promise—the greatest promise of all.

· · · · · · · · · · · ·

A few days later, I take Micah to the park to run off some steam before naptime. He befriends another little hooligan, and together they rambunctiously bang on the musical instruments attached to the jungle gym in the reckless abandon known only to toddlers. I get to chatting with this little guy's mama and am grateful for her casual getup of jean shorts, a t-shirt, and a ponytail. We witness a parent of four close-in-age young ones effortlessly coordinate lunch at the nearby picnic table. Notorious for oversharing with strangers on the regular, I confess to her that I don't know how other women are able to do it with so many kids.

And you know what she says? "I bet a couple of them were accidents!"

Instant soul sisters.

She shares that even though she's too early to show, she's actually pregnant with their second child, and her babies are set to be less than two years apart in age—an accidental surprise for their family. And when I share that I'm in the same boat, I find I'm not the only one who's totally overwhelmed with the prospect of raising two babes.

Life is never what it seems on the surface, is it?

We're still many months away from saying hello to our next little miracle, but my heart is slowly beginning to grow with the promise of our growing family. And that terrifies me!

I don't know if this pregnancy and baby will be healthy. I don't know if I'm going to puke my guts out for weeks on end or if I'll get some relief. I don't know if this child will sleep—sweet Jesus, let them sleep—and I don't know if I'll be any good at raising two children. I don't know if this child will put stress on my marriage, or if my postpartum depression symptoms will rear their ugly head again.

What if I don't have enough love to go around?

What if this hurts my relationship with Micah?

What if this breaks my marriage with Dan?

What if?

What if?

What if?

I confess I seem to be quite fearful. Call it the curse, but when it comes to having and raising babies, fear has been a familiar companion for me. But I do know that I only have one choice in the face of these fears: to let go and trust God.

So this is what I'm praying on repeat: *I surrender to Your will for me, Jesus. I will trust You. Oh Lord, let my faith grow.*

And my family.

August

And So I Write

I should be job searching by now.

The plan was to have my shoulder surgery, get Micah adjusted to part-time preschool (it makes me feel better than saying "daycare"), and focus on physical therapy and recovery for a couple of months. And *then* start to look for a job.

Well, so far, all I have is an outdated résumé and a bit of regret. And it's been months.

Meanwhile, Dan has become a full-time student.

Dan went on sabbatical from his trading career; this is the first time in over a decade that he hasn't been actively following and participating in financial markets. For the past year, he juggled his grad program on top of a full-time job, and our family felt the pressure of his very busy schedule. And believe me, the two of us also found plenty of things to bicker about as a result of the stress.

So after spending the summer serving as head caregiver while I was post-op, in order to finish his grad program more quickly, he transitioned to a full course load to focus solely on school until graduation. And as part of our decision for him to trade his trade for textbooks, we agreed that I'd go back into the professional workforce (at least temporarily) to help pay our bills during this school season.

That was before I knew I was pregnant.

Now it's August and not only am I knocked up, my husband and I are both unemployed, my kid is still attending designer daycare three days a week, and all I seem to be doing with my newly afforded free time is writing and going to physical therapy. And writing, while it may be what is deep within my heart—bursting forth with ease each time I open my laptop—unfortunately doesn't come with a paycheck.

Passion doesn't seem to pay the bills for most of us.

And yet, I write.

When I should be applying.

Dan, my saintly ceaseless supporter, after witnessing my passion to write grow from the ashes this summer, has given me permission to work on my first book instead of interview. Bless him. And in his belief in me, I've allowed myself to dream that there could be a place for me in this world that is all my own. One where purpose and passion meet, and motherhood can also coexist.

I've been more than a little lost.

So here I am. Admitting out loud, for the first time, that I'm a part-time stay-at-home mother with a story in her soul and the spirit to put it on paper. I'm paying for childcare while not getting paid. I'm supporting my husband while he supports our family with the blessing of our savings account and a whole lotta love. I'm probably making some mistakes, but:

I am writing for me.

And for all of us who are trying to find our place in the midst of a world that always seems to have an opinion about our choices. For those of us plagued by the lie that we can't be both good mothers and providers (or perhaps can't be either). For the dreamers who have sacrificed their passions in exchange for obligations. For any of us who are lost without a clue of where we're going.

For you, I write.

For any of us who look at others around us and find ourselves feeling *less than*, I write.

Writing, for me, is a choice to let go, to finally give life to the inner voice that has been so desperate to be heard. To choose to convey life honestly and harness my loads of self-doubt. In my experience, those ingredients welcome grace, camaraderie, and slowly but surely, a belief that I'm worthy of and responsible for something great in this life.

And so I write.

I think the real secret is that we all feel like we're not enough when compared to the impossible expectations we set out for ourselves and for each other. Resting in the knowledge that we're all a bit of a hot mess is when a breakthrough in our own stories can happen—because fear and failure no longer feel so isolating.

And this kind of breakthrough will carve a path to our own individual purpose in this world without questioning its value compared to that of others. Because you are here on purpose.

And for a purpose.

And so I write.

In order to find mine.

And because I have no other choice—to defy it would be to quiet my soul when it demands to be free.

Caution to the Wind

My belly grows bigger with each passing week—my expanding bump reminding us that the countdown to having two children along for the ride is mere months away.

Given my rocky journey into motherhood the first time through—the miscarriage, the wild delivery, the colicky newborn, the feisty bout of depression, our conflict-ridden marriage—I'm fighting with all the energy I've got to enjoy this new pregnancy. Trying with every prayer to protect my mind while carrying my sweet boy. (Yes, it's another boy!) Refusing with all my might to let our joy be stolen.

But my abdomen isn't the only thing expanding at record pace. These days, our family has been met with uncertainty at every turn—leaving me struggling to find my way, more than a little scared to feel so lost.

I wonder, when will the flutter in my womb not mirror the flutter of my anxious heart?

•••••••••••

I've never been the type to "go with the flow."

An ex once told me I need to be more okay with ambiguity in life. I think it was in the middle of one of those infamous D.T.R. talks. You know, the "Define The Relationship" discussions that rarely end well? Well, turns out my concern with his waffling over our future was well-founded. In his case, ambiguity = BIG red flag.

And sure, being okay with ambiguity sounds nice on paper and all. But you know what else is great on paper? Thoroughly managed to-do lists, detailed calendars, and PLANS—perfectly outlined, exhaustively thought out, and properly controlled plans. In my preferred version of the world, there is no plan left behind.

Yet, did you know there are people completely content to navigate life with no road map?

They're the women who hastily throw clothes in a suitcase after work on a Friday and board the first flight they find in order to accept a last-minute invitation to join a friend out of state—abandoning all prior plans for their weekend. They're the girls who are completely okay with being in a years-long relationship—content in their love alone—and don't sweat the belated arrival of a ring or a sincere promise for the future. The ladies who allow nature to take its course as they wait to become pregnant, and then patiently await the arrival of their little miracles without a care in the world, knowing in their hearts that they will deliver healthy, easy children straight out of the womb. The mothers who don't worry about watching for appropriate developmental timelines for their kids' crawling, walking, speech development, potty training—after all, every baby is different.

I know these people exist in the world. But as I've finally come to accept, I'm not one of them. While they embody a carefree nature and whimsical worldview, I'm forced to actively manage my biologically anxious brain with regular counseling and monitored medication. I praise God for professionals.

But on the brink of another baby and with so many other worries on the horizon, I covet those women's peace, and dream of their assuredness.

I wonder if this time around I could become one of those women who so easily throws caution to the wind?

•••••••••••

Long before smartphones and Google Maps, a group of friends and I set out on a road trip to the beautiful state of Minnesota for a mutual friend's summer wedding. We raided Trader Joe's for an array of road-trip-worthy snacks, set up a playlist on an ancient iPod, and pressed "print" for our MapQuest directions.

Elbow-deep in a bag of edamame in the back seat, I cradled our paper copy of the route between my legs—a poorly chosen placemat for my snacking. Having accumulated soybean shells *en masse*, I rolled down the window to discard my biodegradable remnants, only to have our only map fly away with my trash.

I had literally thrown caution to the wind, much to my travel companions' chagrin.

•••••••••••

From what I can tell, the God I love has a wildly imaginative sense of humor—He shocked the heck out of our family with the news of this pregnancy. From the moment I peed on that stick, He plucked my carefully curated calendar right out of my tightly wound fingers and threw our family into a season of complete and utter ambiguity, with no destination in sight (except for a labor and delivery room sometime this spring).

And in addition to the mess of being knocked up unexpectedly, the list of other questions keeps coming.

Where are we going to live once our lease expires and we're forced to move? *No clue.* Where and what will my husband be doing for a job when he graduates from his Master's program in May? *Really not sure.* How the heck am I going to raise two babies at the same time? *Wish I could tell you.* And most importantly, when will we have the answers to these really important questions?

Your guess is as good as mine.

As you can imagine, this season of uncertainty has been more than a little difficult for a woman with an ever-worried heart—especially while preparing for another human being's earthly arrival.

All we know for sure is that a change in direction is ahead—and for me, change has always been a hard turn to take.

So standing at the cusp of more crossroads than I'd like to see before me, all I can choose is how I respond to what lies ahead. I wonder, can I fight to focus on the truths I know rather than the worries that plague me?

●●●●●●●●●●●

Wending our way through Wisconsin, we only talked about the lost map once. Rather than berate me for making such a stupid mistake—I might have done the same, had the roles been reversed—my go-with-the-flow friends laughed at my oversight and aimed our vehicle in the general direction of Minneapolis. Rather than follow a step-by-step guide—long gone to the wind—we did our best to read the road signs and turned up the volume on the speakers for the rest of the ride.

That sunny afternoon, as we meandered towards our destination, we bonded over intense rounds of "Truth or Dare" and sang Billy Joel at the top of our lungs. When our snacks ran out, we pulled over at a rundown brat stop that served the best cheddarwurst I've ever tasted.

And we laughed.

When we felt our heads spinning—not knowing where to go next—we asked for directions, calling for help when we had to.

And you know what?

We made it to our final stop—and with fewer wrong turns than you'd expect. I'd bargain we had more fun getting there that way, a lost map turning what could have been a boring tour of western Wisconsin into a spontaneous adventure. Looking at that trip through my rearview mirror, I can see that though our route took a few unexpected turns, it brought along some beautiful views—ones we would have missed otherwise.

And from that unplanned winding road, I learned that just because you don't know exactly how or when you'll arrive somewhere, it doesn't mean you won't get there. It just means you have to move forward, make one decision at a time, and course-correct as needed.

And maybe you order yourself a cheddarwurst when the urge strikes.

• • • • • • • • • • • •

I wish I could wrap up this season of unknowns by writing a clear game plan for our lives—a plan that will get us from a state of utter disarray to a fully functional family of four. I dream of presenting a step-by-step manual to my worried self.

See, love? This is how it's all going to work out. Everything will be just fine.

Instead, God is having me sit in the backseat for this one.

In this season, He's giving me—us—a chance to wait on Him to lead the way. I don't like being pulled from the driver's seat one bit, but sometimes we have no other choice. Maybe when it's all over, I'll get to see how He showed up, mapping out our lives in the wonderful way only He can do. And maybe next time the winds of change force their way into our lives, I won't be so concerned with how to get from here to there, instead trusting in His providence.

If I were a betting woman, I'd bargain that I'll always struggle to go with the flow; throwing caution to the wind is just not in my nature. But maybe there's a part of my nature that I can hold on to a bit more tightly—the part of me that knows the way to the truth.

October

Fire

It's one of those rare perfect days as a family. Our Indian summer has finally begun to wane, and with it, cooler temperatures have rolled in. Bundled up in sweatshirts and jeans, we set off to the apple orchard to enjoy a perfectly sunny morning with Dan's brother and sister-in-law and Micah's adorable cousin, Lucy, only three months his junior.

We pick overpriced Honeycrisps and give Micah the chance to finally climb aboard a "tra-too" (tractor), his latest toddler obsession. We lunch on Wisconsin brats and cold apple cider and leave with lofty intentions to bake away our pickings. Micah's behavior convinces all the strangers of our incredible parenting skills, and the moment he's buckled into his car seat, he passes out so we can enjoy a quiet ride back to the city.

Upon arrival, after unloading our goods, Dan shuttles off to the gym with Micah in tow, and I relish an opportunity for an afternoon nap for no reason other than, simply, I can.

It's glorious.

We end the day sharing pizza and pasta at a favorite neighborhood eatery and wander home slowly—until someone's dirty diaper makes haste our return.

Truly, a better day couldn't have been had.

With an early bedtime for Micah and a husband scrambling to finish some nearly-due grad school homework, I find myself standing in my quiet (and clean) kitchen that Saturday night, savoring the sweet memories we captured for our little family that day. As I take in the sounds of the city through my open kitchen window—the El train crossing on the tracks overhead, the muffled conversation of my neighbors on their back deck, a dog's bark in the distance—I close my eyes and thank God for giving us such beauty together.

With a soft breeze gently cooling my face, the overwhelming smell of a nearby campfire cuts through the darkness. An uncommon treat for city life, the night has brought with it my favorite smell in the entire world and God's clearest voice to my heart.

I close my eyes and allow myself to breathe in the memories of fires familiar.

In and out.

In and out.

In and out.

The flames dance every time.

They're tied to my soul irrevocably and bring forth deep meaning in their memory.

Even years later, I will thank God the fire always brings me back to this day. This perfect day in the starting story of our lives. A husband, a child, a family.

An everlasting fire growing in my heart.

November
To My Micah

Micah has always been a terrible sleeper. Like, really bad.

So when I insist on sneaking into his room at 5:45 in the morning to give him a quick goodbye kiss and say a prayer over his little body before heading to the airport, you can imagine that Dan isn't too thrilled. Never mind that I already took the chance to rock that sweet child to sleep last night.

Twice.

But a mama's heart can only withstand so much, and mine requires that I properly say farewell to my baby before taking off to the west coast for an overdue weekend away with some girlfriends. In my defense, it's only my second trip away from him since birth, and I'm addicted to smothering those chubby cheeks with my love.

For the record, he typically sleeps until 7 AM—which defines a late morning in his book—so I'm clearly light on my feet and as quiet as a mouse.

You're welcome, sweetheart.

As I reflect on my frantic need to soak up every possible second with my son, I realize that I've started the slow process of grieving. Of saying goodbye to these precious moments where I can quietly kiss my sleeping baby. Where my sweet boy can fit his entire little body in the space of my lap. Where he falls asleep effortlessly with just the comfort of my arms (and, let's be honest, also the help of a pitch-black bedroom, an industrial strength sound machine, an ironclad bedtime routine, and a healthy dousing of essential oils). Where I'm the first person he runs to in moments of joy, pain, fear—or in his insatiable desire to tackle everyone in his presence.

Where I am his everything and he is mine.

For the past twenty-eight months, we have been one—two people inextricably connected. We shared a body, and a life source, and then a heart. And I'm not ready for that to change.

I'm afraid to see the chub of his cheeks fade to reveal features more boy than baby. I worry that my arms—and my lap—will no longer be big enough to be his favorite spot. I fear a time when he'll have the words to communicate his needs to the world, because I will no longer have the responsibility to answer every one of them on instinct alone.

I wonder if I'll stop seeing them so clearly?

And I reject the idea that a day will come when he would rather not let his Mama give him a kiss—especially in front of his friends.

Oh Lord, I'm not ready for any of these things to change.

But change is coming.

I watch in awe as my baby transforms into a child. He's become obsessed with farm equipment—literally obsessed—loves playing with anything on wheels, and for reasons I cannot understand, he passionately adores cats. I see his brain firing on all cylinders: new words, gestures, and comprehension developing every day. And I'm witnessing his not-so-little personality coming alive. Don't get in the way of that boy and his mission to find trouble wherever he goes!

Oh Jesus, he will be so much more than my heart could have hoped. I am one thankful Mama.

But change is coming—in more ways than one.

By the grace of love, a new life has begun. As my sweet boy lays his head on my shoulder and wraps his tiny arms around my neck, his body blankets another. I can feel the faint flutter of our new little one's existence in between us—a soft reminder that he'll be a part of this place of comfort soon, too.

And as my belly grows—slowly increasing the physical distance between our heartbeats—it feels as if Micah has already moved farther from me. How can I make sure he knows my love for him will never know distance? That nothing could ever come between us?

I already know that what they say is true—your love doesn't halve; your heart just doubles in size. But will my first baby understand that? Will he remain secure as the tides of change make waves in our little family? Is it possible to be what both my children need at the same time?

Will my love be enough?

But change is coming—and soon our family will be four.

So, as the calendar counts down the days until the baby's arrival, my prayer is that my Micah will never question his place in my heart. I hope with all my might that he'll love his brother as ferociously as he loves us. And I ask the Lord to bless all three of us with larger hearts.

Because I just know this new little life will take our breath away—and our hearts along with it.

So as his little brother grows into our family, I want my son to know that even though he will soon share my heart, he'll never have less of it.

Micah, sweet boy, you have helped me become more than I knew I could be. You have given me a more tender heart, a deeper understanding of the Father's love, a fuller life in every way, and a stronger ability to survive on less sleep.

Your little life may have rocked my world when it began, but I would have it no other way.

My sincerest prayer is that you will never question whether my arms are big enough to comfort you. Because of my love for you, I finally understand the definition of unconditional—there is nothing you could do that would take my heart from you. Know that

I will carry your joy, pain, fear. And I will always be here for all your moments—the big, the insignificant, the beautiful, the hard.

Change may be coming, but we'll always share a heart.

And you, my love, will always have to give your Mama a kiss. Even if your friends are around.

December

Growing Life
(With a Side of Bitterness)

It's a rare afternoon for us. I've managed to squeeze my bulging belly and growing thighs into some borrowed maternity spandex and laced up my tennis shoes. I'm on a mission to get a little exercise before stealing a hot shower at our beloved health club while Micah enjoys the kids' club for ninety minutes. Clocking in at twenty-five pounds heavier than a few months ago and still gingerly gaining back my physical abilities after my shoulder surgery, I grab a couple free weights and set up to do a few rounds of light lifting and cardio (read: walk-waddle the track in slow motion while simultaneously sweating like a cow).

Just as I'm wrapping up my final round of feigning fit, a kindly older gentleman interrupts my set of five-pound presses to inquire if I should be doing such things in my condition. He proceeds to pepper me with questions about my baby-baking body and draws plenty of unwanted attention to my previously private corner of the gym.

Embarrassed, I scurry to the women's locker room and grab the three mini towels it takes to dry my heaving mass. Then I take a quick shower in the back corner of the locker room—my favored hideaway from the potential eyes of the skinnier, baby-free other women.

Earlier this week, while conspicuously making our way through the Chipotle line—Micah's impatience for chicken tacos growing in sync with my own annoyance at parenting a whining toddler—the young, smiley server noticed out loud my obvious state of about-to-popness and reminded me *again* that I really was as big as a beached whale—just one with a penchant for Mexican food.

Then, there's the needing to buy bigger maternity clothes.

The regular vagina-stabbing pains of my pubic bone separating.

The inability to put on my shoes or my rings or my dignity.

And the ever-present lower back pain.

All of it reminds me that my body is completely out of my control and not even a little bit my own. It steals the joy of pregnancy at every turn.

I promised myself that this time around, I'd drink in the experience of growing a baby and savor the miracle of creating life. But all I can seem to do is quench my thirst for sugar-full lemonade and meet my craving for endless tubs of mint chip. In fact, I've said to Dan at least three hundred times since peeing on that dang stick that I will NEVER do this again. Don't you DARE do this to me again!

Safe to say, I'm not one of those women that just loves being pregnant. Enter the early stages of Mom guilt and self-loathing—and way too much bitterness.

I keep telling myself that this is just a season and this too shall pass, but man, this funk is sticking. Bitterness has a way of creeping into the crevices of your heart and staying there, doesn't it? I'm bitter and lonely in it. I realize I've become someone I'm not a huge fan of, but I'm unable to figure out how to get back to the woman I want to be—for my 1.9 kids, for my marriage, for myself.

I stand in that little back corner gym shower and let the piping hot water hit my back as I cradle my baby belly. While I hold my growing child, a familiar Bible verse bubbles up in my heart and begins its repeated cadence in my mind.

But the fruit of the Spirit is love, joy, peace, patience, kindness,

goodness, faithfulness, gentleness, self-control; against such things there is no law.
Galatians 5:22-23

The fruits of the spirit.

Man, I really need some of that fruit in my life. That is the woman I want to be. A woman who has so much love and joy and peace. Who could be described as patient with her children and kind to the stranger. Whose goodness and faithfulness enrich her marriage and her family. A mother with a gentle heart and a wife with self-control.

But the fruits of the spirit seem to have been spoiled by the bitterness of this angry pregnant lady.

As my arms circle my growing belly, I think about how becoming a mother has been the most amazing experience of my life—and I'm being blessed to experience it all over again. In spite of the challenges of carrying a baby, I get the privilege of bearing fruit in the form of new life—and that will surely produce more fruit in my spirit than I could produce alone.

But only if I let it.

So, Lord, would you help this bitter heart see some fruit? I know it's there.

Love? I don't love the not-so-fun physical demands of pregnancy, but I've never loved any human being more purely than Micah. I'm certain this next child will be responsible for adding more love in my life than I deserve.

Joy? I'm not overjoyed that I have to carry this load—all while my husband's six-pack is preserved. But joy? You have no idea what joy is until you watch a little person see bubbles for the first time. Kids are capable of feeling unadulterated joy with a frequency that adults are just lucky to be able to witness.

Peace? It's been a while since my heart has been at peace. But the Zoloft is helping me access the calm a bit more easily this time through. I can't wait for the moment they place this baby in my arms and I get to bring immediate peace to a soul in the form of an embrace. My mama superpower? My arms now give peace. What a gift I get to give!

Patience? While I know my patience will be tested in every way as I parent these boys—blowouts, temper tantrums, the child-sized cart at Trader Joe's—you can't get better at something without a little practice. I'm learning that patience will grow as my expectations of perfection—or efficient trips to the grocery store—decrease. And trust me, there's nothing about my motherhood that is perfect.

Kindness? I'm growing in my love of kindness each time I teach my two-year-old how to share toys with his little friends. There's nothing like a fight over a train table at the library to highlight the sinful hearts innate in us all. Each time I encourage Micah to be kind and to love well and to wait his turn, I remind myself of the same commission: to treat others with kindness and to sacrifice my own desires for the sake of others.

Goodness? For me, there isn't much that seems good about pregnancy. I recognize the honor and privilege of carrying my children, but I just don't like the process; I feel awful through the whole thing, and it feels like nine months drags on forever. But babies are the actual definition of goodness in the world. And I get two of them—so much more goodness than I deserve.

Faithfulness? This has always been a bit tricky. Being faithful to what's important—the Lord, my husband, my family—gets a little lost when I get caught up with me. But motherhood has unburied a selflessness that hasn't come naturally otherwise. And because it is so darn exhausting, it has also helped narrow my focus a bit; I don't have any energy left for the little things anymore. I'm praying that I can continue to grow in my faithfulness to the meaningful as I'm forced to die to the selfish.

Gentleness? Again, this is new for me. Before my boys, I'm not sure anyone would have called me gentle. In fact, my best friends in the world have voted me most likely to win if the Hunger Games were a real thing. I've spent most of my life harnessing my physical, big, competitive personality into a likeable female-sized box. But one of my sweetest memories is when my own mom would softly stroke my hair, just grazing my forehead with her light touch as I lay my head in her lap when I was tired, sick, or scared. And even as an adult, I conjure up this image and attempt to center my heart on the memory of her gentleness when I find myself feeling fearful or overwhelmed (or on an airplane). So for my boys, I'll snuggle as much as possible. I'll cradle them every chance I get. And I'll stroke their foreheads with the gentle touch of love that I learned from the best mother I know. It may be new for me, but gentleness is one attribute I'm excited to perfect.

Self-control? Is it even possible for a super-pregnant woman to pretend to have self-control when the dessert menu arrives? Not this sugar-crazy mama. But even I can say no to my beloved caffeine and wine habits in the interest of caring for my unborn children—proof that one version of self-control has shown up in spades.

So love, joy, peace, patience, kindness, goodness, gentleness and self-control: maybe the fruits of the spirit aren't as far away from me as I thought. Lord, until this baby finally gets his eviction notice, I pray for more fruit than bitterness.

Against such things there is no law.

Speaking of laws, I would like to take this moment to remind the general population of the unwritten law against commenting on a pregnant woman's condition. I know I'm huge. I know I waddle and make lifting five-pound weights appear to be a Herculean effort. I know I don't look like I need that extra side of guac, but I'm creating an actual person in here.

An actual person.

Christmas Eve

Ready

The red maternity dress I'm wearing has to be the least flattering garment ever, but it does a decent job of proclaiming the festive season. My boys have obediently worn khakis and button-downs and we managed to leave the house with little complaint—and almost on time. With the church nursery doors closed for the holiday service, we've stocked the diaper bag with an assortment of Micah's favorite snacks and loaded up the iPad with new episodes of *Elmo's World*, determined to see the whole sermon in spite of inevitable judgment for being *those* technology-dependent parents.

As we settle into the dusty balcony pew—proof of its rare use in our small growing church—I struggle not to let my disappointment show on my face. My vision of Christmas Eves past—nights with my sisters and parents in our Sunday best and ready to enjoy a lavish meal after a reverent candlelit service—have been exchanged for an ill-fitting red tent dress, a morning family-friendly service, and the high-pitched crooning of Elmo competing with the holiday hymns, a welcome exchange for occupying my toddler.

As our pastor digs into the well-known story of a Savior being born in a manger, I struggle to center my heart on the Christmas story—the humble and beautiful beginning of it all. Instead, I recall the struggle of the past year, one full of emotional and physical lows, more conflict within my marriage than I care to admit, and a whole lot of fear over a number of unknowns still on our family's horizon.

To say I'm not in the Christmas spirit is an understatement.

And yet my attention is drawn back to our preacher below—his voice breaking through my ugly inner tirade. Is it me or did he just take a left turn from the narrative that's worn tracks in my memory of Christmas services? Rather than dive into the familiar tale of the culminating joy of a long-awaited birth, he brings forth the story of the shepherds instead, the lowly servants watching over their flock at night and the first to hear the Good News that a Savior was to be born in Bethlehem. I learn that at that time, shepherds faithfully raised sheep, preparing them for slaughter to serve as the blameless atonements of the Jewish people in sacrifice to their God. And yet, they were unable to meet the standards of remaining blameless themselves—shepherds were considered less than in more ways than one.

Oh, how I can relate.

But it was to these men—these less-than-the-rest men—that the angel of the Lord first appeared, breaking through the darkness with the news of the true Light. To these unworthy few, God showed up first.

And His news blew them away.

An angel of the Lord appeared to them, and the glory of the Lord shone around them, and they were terrified. But the angel said to them, "Do not be afraid. I bring you good news that will cause great joy for all the people. Today in the town of David a Savior has been born to you; he is the Messiah, the Lord. This will be a sign to you: You will find a baby wrapped in cloths and lying in a manger."

Suddenly a great company of the heavenly host appeared with the angel, praising God and saying,

"Glory to God in the highest heaven,
and on earth peace to those on whom his favor rests."
Luke 2: 9-14

And on earth, peace to those on whom His favor rests.

Peace? Well it's certainly been a while. Favor? I mean probably, but it sure doesn't feel like it.

And in this moment, our pastor interrupts my thoughts again with a quiet question, "Are there any of you here that have had just a disaster of a year?"

YES.

Me.

He pauses.

"I want you to know you are not alone. Would you stand so we can pray for you?"

And without realizing it, I'm rising to my feet.

Apparently I'm not alone—I stand with quite a few others in the congregation who've seen better days. And with a soft voice, our pastor looks upon our tired faces and invites us into the Christmas story. He reminds us that in the midst of it all—the feeling less-than, the trauma, the fear, the disappointment—God wants us to hear the Good News too, and know that He has a place for us in that stable even when we've told ourselves we aren't enough. We'll always be welcome.

That on earth, there is peace to those on whom His favor rests.

And as his gentle words speak to my soul—a long-awaited salve to my fractured and angry heart—I hear God inviting me into a season of renewal, a time for healing and joy and promise. He tells me He has so much more for me than I can see.

And I bow my head as the tears stream down my cheeks.

When I look up, my sweet boys are holding hands, and my kind husband offers me a knowing half-smile. As I wipe the evidence of my emotions from my face, I lean my head on his shoulder and cradle my growing baby belly. Our second son kicks for attention, reminding me that soon he's going to be a part of the beautiful, imperfect story of our family. And I look upon the cross below and take a deep, hopeful breath.

This year I'm ready for renewal to happen. This year, I'm ready to seek the joy.

And this Christmas Eve morning, sitting on a dusty pew bench wearing an oversized red maternity dress next to the two boys I love most in the world and with the third well on his way, I realize that in order to claim the renewal for which I so deeply yearn, I need to let go. I need to accept myself for the mother that I am, not the mother I thought I would or should be.

Oh Lord, renew a right spirit within me. Break me free.

PART THREE: REFLECTING

New Roots

5th grade

I never expected to get such life-changing news that night—family dinners were typically best for sharing stories and catching up on our days. But when Dad announced that our family was moving across state lines for his big new job opportunity, my parents did their best to make it sound like an adventure: a bigger house, a better school, new friends. As boxes were packed and our house was sold, my two sisters and I looked forward to arriving in eastern Pennsylvania, where exciting new experiences awaited us—our childish ignorance masking any fears for the huge change coming our way.

When I walked into our new elementary school, I soon realized the struggle before me. On top of having to navigate the shark-infested waters of a "foreign" lunchroom, I found myself assigned to advanced classes; in sixth grade this was the equivalent of social torture.

With my parents' encouragement, I signed up for as many groups and clubs as one kid could—ski club, Girl Scouts, choir, lacrosse, youth group—and slowly I found my way. Both to new friends and to the safety of a new familiar. Though I shed many tears as I longed for the security of my previous life, eventually new memories were being written on the walls of my heart.

New roots had sprouted.

•••••••••••

10th grade

Another huge change loomed on the horizon for our family, much to my surprise. When Dad came home early from work one day during my sophomore year, he announced the shocking news that he'd taken another new role, this time in Chicago. Again, my parents did their best to make it sound like an adventure—a bigger house, a better school, new friends—but I knew better. As boxes were packed, I dreaded our family's winter arrival in Illinois—I now had a very clear picture of the challenges this change would bring, and I wanted nothing to do with them.

When I found myself walking through the front doors of Naperville North High School—smack dab in the middle of my high school experience—I floundered. Making friends was hard, I constantly felt out of place, and I was angry at my parents for sentencing me to live out my high school days in a social prison without a girls' lacrosse team. But eventually I managed to secure a few friendships that would keep me above water until graduation, when I could decide for myself where to go next.

Turns out new roots can still grow in dry dirt.

•••••••••••

Freshman year of college

A blur of green greeted me as my Dad rounded the turn into the main drive and I caught sight of Wittenberg University for the first time. Summer was in the air and the perfectly manicured campus pulsed with new life—students in backpacks trudging to class, lounging on blankets soaking in the afternoon sun, and chasing Frisbees across the sprawling lawn.

Leaning out the passenger window of the minivan, I breathed it all in: *college.*

As Dad was pulling into the queue with all the other vehicles bursting at the seams with the belongings of nervous students, I felt more excited for a fresh start than fearful of a new unknown.

Unpacking in record time—my Dad bribed a couple boys to help move me in—I kissed my family goodbye and sat down on my freshly made bunk with a sense of resolve. This would be the place I'd put my stake in the ground—a place of my very own choosing.

Seasoned at the whole new-school gig, I put on my favorite Abercrombie sweatsuit skirt and platform foam sandals, threw my student lanyard around my neck, and started walking door-to-door on a mission to introduce myself to future friends. Thankfully, I didn't have to go very far; every girl I met was just as eager to find her new place as I was. And by the time the orientation assembly was underway, I wasn't alone anymore.

This time, I planted new roots myself.

••••••••••••

First year of adult life

After four fantastic years in college, my sorority sisters and I were searching for our "what's next." In the spirit of the saleswoman I was soon to become on paper, I convinced three of my dearest friends that our lives would be more fun in the Windy City—especially if we all moved there together!

So that second semester of senior year, four of us piled into my 1997 Chevy Lumina— "The Blue Barracuda"—and drove five hours through Indiana to find ourselves a big-city apartment for life, post-graduation. A month later, on a whim and a prayer—diplomas still fresh in hand—we moved our mismatched, secondhand furniture into an apartment that was a lot smaller than it had seemed at lease-signing.

In our naiveté, two of us had zero jobs, three of us slept for a year in a basement with no real windows or insulation, and all four of us learned that the big city could also be a harsh place for the wandering. But side-by-side, we began to find our way: to securing gainful employment, to navigating public transportation, to finding a church home. And after surviving a tough first year together, it felt like Chicago was becoming ours.

New roots sure grow more quickly with friends to help you dig in.

••••••••••••

November, late twenties

We sat in his living room talking well into the night—something we'd done many times since summer—and I wondered if things between us would ever develop. Tired of living in that gray space familiar to any Millennial who's had a crush and a Netflix account, I'd been hoping for months that he would find the courage to ask me out.

As I gathered my coat and purse to leave, he paused and startled me by inviting me to join him for drinks the following week.

Finally.

I remember clearly what I wore that fateful Tuesday: heeled black booties with my favorite oversized magenta scarf atop a fitted blazer. As we sat drinking craft beers in a cozy bar on a cold November night, I found myself wondering if this date was both a first and a last.

Perhaps new roots could take hold in your heart?

••••••••••••

Two months later

I fell in love with him in a Wendy's parking lot.

Because Dan has always believed in making all my dreams come true, he drove me to pick up some spicy chicken nuggets and a junior Frosty after my particularly hard day of work. And as we shared fries and talked about our day—all while wearing sweatpants—I realized right then that I would choose him.

I would always choose him.

It would take twelve more months for him to get down on one knee, but as our lives merged together that year—one family birthday party, one Sunday morning church service, and one flag football game at a time—his presence became the constant I could count on. And his actions continued to say to my scarred heart: *I choose you.*

And on a hot August day that following summer, I vowed to choose him forever.

This time, new roots came with a new name.

• • • • • • • • • • • •

April, Age 30

I like to joke that Northwestern's Prentice Women's Hospital is the Ritz-Carlton of Labor & Delivery. We had a view of the lake, floor-to-ceiling windows, gourmet chicken salad a phone call away, and round-the-clock professional help available at the press of the button.

So leaving the five-star hospital experience with a colicky newborn to return to a condo with paper-thin walls and childless neighbors only amplified the stress of parenting. Our affection for our urban dwelling quickly waned as the sleepless nights of pacifying a screaming child compounded.

We began asking ourselves the question: *Do we need to make new roots somewhere else?*

• • • • • • • • • • • •

Spring with a one-year-old

It would take a desperate move to a townhouse in the city to help us survive Micah's arrival in our lives. In exchange for a small fortune each month, we found thick brick walls that provided a much-needed buffer from our new neighbors, and a finished basement and small backyard promised that we could both enjoy city life and give our son ample space to play.

We'd found a way to make it all work—or so we thought.

When our landlords sprang the news that they weren't going to renew our lease—only weeks after learning we'd be welcoming another child in the spring—we were left with a big decision to make. It was the decision we'd been avoiding for longer than we cared to admit:

Would we finally be planting new roots in the suburbs?

• • • • • • • • • • •

March 1st, very pregnant

I'm eight months pregnant and I'm watching the movers wrap plastic around everything we own from my spread-eagle perch on our low kitchen stool, my half-caf Starbucks in one hand and a bagel in the other. I just got back from dropping Micah off for his last day of daycare, and Dan has got to be around here somewhere.

In my typical fashion, I'm avoiding thinking of the day (*weeks, months, years...*) before us and focusing on the things I can control now: starting with my breakfast. But as I supervise the packing of our house (read: shoving carbs down my throat while four men sweat their tushies off doing everything), my brain can't help but remind me of the radical change we've signed up for—and that's in addition to our baby boy's impending arrival:

We're actually moving to the suburbs.

Every long-term urban dweller has watched the same exodus of families chasing cheaper rent once children have come onto the scene. If they don't run right away, it definitely happens by kindergarten—when it's time to pass the problems of inner-city schools onto someone else. Sure, some people find a way, but is living within the city limits worth the higher cost of living for our family of four?

Probably not.

Do we want to be financially burdened in order to maintain our city lifestyle—and all that comes with it—on Dan's single income?

Sounds really stressful.

Would living down the street from grandparents make stay-at-home-mom life better?

You know it.

So after living in the city for nearly eleven years—and dragging my feet on making this decision for at least two of them—I'm saying goodbye to the first chapter of my adulthood.

And instead, I'm saying hello to our new home just an hour north of Chicago; a big (for us) brick house in Dan's hometown in Lake County.

I'm praying these new roots are just what our growing family needs to thrive.

Late March

Joining

"Babe. Babe. BABE! Wake up!"

I jab Dan in the ribs, and he rolls over and rubs his eyes. "What is it?"

"It's happening! I've been tracking them and they've been coming regularly, only a couple minutes apart."

"Are you sure?"

"YES. I've been through this before. Stop questioning me. Call your freaking mom."

I am well known for my ability to stay calm and pleasant under stress.

He reaches for his phone, and I brace for another contraction. After it fades, I grab my sweatshirt from the floor and shuffle into the bathroom to brush my teeth. I shove my toiletries and glasses into my overnight bag and lean over the bathroom counter as another tightening of my abdomen stops me in my tracks.

"Are your parents on their way yet? How long 'til they get here?"

Dan joins me in the bathroom and frantically gathers everything he needs: a toothbrush, a phone charger, a change of underwear.

We've been through this before, so we know the drill—the items to grab, the pains ahead of me. Except this time we have a sleeping toddler down the hall and a fifteen-mile drive through the suburbs ahead of us.

My anxiety over the possibility of delivering a baby in my bathtub increases as the minutes tick by.

"Come on. They should be here any minute," he promises.

While Dan warms up the car and loads our bags, I take deep breaths and count contractions. I wait for my in-laws, doubled over a kitchen chair, and lament that soon I'll be standing braless in my father-in-law's presence. I doubt he'll notice, but in the name of keeping that awkwardness from our lives, I hope to make our time together brief.

"Hi there," my mother-in-law says as she comes through the front door. She lovingly rubs my back. "How are you doing?"

"Hanging in there. Just hoping this will be fast," I reply.

"You don't look too bad!" she expertly notes.

I can see what she's thinking on her face: this is a false alarm and we woke her up in the middle of the night for nothing. I start to question the severity of the cramping as I walk with moderate ease to the car, noting that the last time we raced to the hospital I could barely breathe. Once I'm safely settled in my seat on an old beach towel, Dan slams the driver's side door and peels out of the driveway, memories of my record-paced delivery of Micah at the forefront of his mind.

He promised me he wouldn't let me deliver a baby in the back seat, and he is a man of his word. Yet as we fly down the highway, I notice the cramping subsiding. I choose to say nothing.

When I get dropped at the front door of the hospital in sync with another laboring mother, I offer to let her check in before me; her pain is so palpable, her moans so guttural—and in that moment, I know: I'll be going back home soon.

A few hours of monitoring later—pains subsiding as time passes—we're back home with Micah and I find myself tired, impatient, and embarrassed.

How could I get it wrong? How much longer do I have to wait? Why do I hate being pregnant so much?

I just want to meet my son.

• • • • • • • • • • •

April 10th (Labor & Delivery)

"How big is he?" I shout across the labor and delivery room.

"NINE POUNDS, TEN OUNCES!"

"I knew it! Man, that was freaking awful! I'm so glad it's over." I notice my OB's side-eye to the nurse and correct, "I'm so glad he's here and he's healthy. Isn't he beautiful?"

But who are they to judge? They watched what just happened to my body while my giant baby came tearing into this world.

I'm allowed to admit that was awful, goshdarnit.

Since my not-so-little nine-pounder kept baking until my thirty-nine-week induction date, my mom had come to our house to stay with Micah, a fact that eased my anxiety about making it to the delivery room in time. And even better, we arrived at our room with enough time for me to eat a bagel and drink a coffee before they hooked me up to the IV and started pumping me with Pitocin.

Thankfully, the hospital has HGTV—a luxury I was forced to give up when Dan convinced me we should ditch cable a couple years ago—and I was thrilled to discover a *Fixer Upper* marathon was underway.

Nothing like a little Joanna Gaines to get a girl in the mood to have a baby.

A couple hours in, I started to feel a bit uncomfortable and I called for my epidural—settling in to enjoy my peaceful, medicated, and planned labor and delivery.

Yet things never seem to go just as you hope, do they?

Long (seven-hour-total) story short, my epidural lost its mojo by the crowning moment and my screams scared the kid-free women on the floor into never having sex again.

And, knowing I was sad he didn't take pictures after my first delivery, Dan got the entire show on camera—down to the very last vein on the umbilical cord. Let's just say if you were to play through the slideshow of our birth, you'd recommend I get a bikini wax.

But I survived. We survived.

And my beautiful baby boy is here and he's healthy. Thank you, Jesus.

The first time I held him, I whispered, "Oh, hello, sweet Levi. Happy birthday. We've been waiting for you to join us."

Now, while my OB stitches me up, I send our family an update on his arrival. I decide to leave out the down-and-dirty details of my failed-to-properly-work epidural and the repeat second-degree tear, and instead attach a picture of our beautiful baby boy.

Levi Cross is here!

He's joining us forever. Whether he likes it or not.

Made for More

Ring of fire
So I guess that's a thing
Life breaking through
While breaking me
Looks just like him
We sure have a brand
9 pounds 10 ounces
No wonder
Tears of relief
To be relieved of his carrying
And yet,
Hasn't that just begun?
Heart exploding
Grief retreating
From the fear of multiplying
While also dividing
Nervous heart and shaking hands
Kneeling with open arms
For our first to run back home
His innocence quickly fading in comparison
In profile, they are mirror images of one another
Head-on, a contrast more pronounced:
The first a blue so clear you can see the ocean floor
The next a milky chocolate brown
Two children make more our family
And siblings forged forever
How we never knew
We were made for more: four

Fourth Trimester

Rain, Rain, Go Away.

I'm convinced there's a shade of green that can only be seen on rainy days. As if God in His infinite wisdom chose to find a small way to brighten our days because He knows that, as the rain moves in, it often brings a bit of disappointment along.

Of loss.

Of changed expectations.

Rain tends to ruin plans for a day spent outside. It has a habit of increasing traffic on morning commutes. It often requires an unwanted midweek mowing of the lawn—thankfully, a chore that gets assigned to my husband. Rain can flood basements; it can ruin your favorite pair of shoes; and in my experience, it *always* makes for a very cranky, cooped-up toddler and his sunshine-loving Mama.

But have you noticed that, as the rain comes pouring down, it magically unearths a color so vibrant it offsets the gray? It highlights the trees, the grass, the leaves in a shade of green that distracts from the wet. A heavenly attempt to try and liven up the mood.

As if to remind us that with the rain comes life, bursting forth in glorious green.

And yet, rainy days are still not my favorite.

This morning is no different. As I struggle through my first cup of coffee and episode of *Daniel Tiger*—all while nursing a six-week-old baby—I stare out the window as sheets and sheets of rain hit the deck—*again*—and think about how much harder life will be today because of the tempestuous forecast, a constant for the past week.

In my brewing—both literally and figuratively—I barely notice the shock of green enveloping my backyard.

Forget about running a bunch of overdue errands with a newborn in tow. Screw trying to check out that new park after school to burn off loads of little-boy energy. Hard pass at attempting to do my hair when it will just get ruined anyway.

As I sip, I mutter, "Rain, rain, go away. Come again another day."

I send Micah off to school in his ratty old sneakers—surely a futile attempt to preserve his one pair of decent shoes this season—and I instantly regret not buying him a much-needed pair of new Dinosaur rain boots for his love of puddle jumping. But neglecting to supply appropriate rain gear for my adventurous toddler to wear to his pro-play-outside-in-the-mud Montessori preschool is the least of my oversights these days.

Last week I left our brand-new-to-us designer stroller in the middle of the mall parking lot. This was after a depressing attempt to find a dress in which to squeeze my postpartum, record-sized body for our good friends' fancy downtown wedding. Yesterday, I barely got a text sent off in time to acknowledge a best friend's birthday before the day transformed into tomorrow: too little and too late. And let's not mention the loads of laundry that have sat, damp, in the washer—my repeated neglect a surefire way to ruin those good towels we finally invested in when we bought our house.

Three days last week Micah showed up at school without his mandatory pre-applied sunblock or sun hat. And please don't count the days that frozen chicken nuggets and microwavable macaroni and cheese are the only things standing between me and a so-called dinner for one hangry little boy.

But more than my failure to keep an organized and prepared version of our life going—each small lapse in memory adding up to equal our family's new status quo of chaos since Levi's birth—I'd forgotten how easy it is to forget yourself when your life revolves around a newborn baby (and his brother) every waking hour of every day and night.

I should have done a better job mentally preparing for the guaranteed storm that comes with newborn life.

The addition of a new baby to our household nearly broke us the first time around. At least that's how Dan and I tend to remember Micah's entrance into the world and into our family. Poor thing. Hopefully the passage of time will soften the memory of those brutal first weeks (months, year), but truth be told, he really kicked us in the teeth. Thankfully he's grown into the most amazing toddler, and the endless videos of his hilarious shenanigans prove it. I promise you, the traits that made Micah a miserable baby have made him the coolest kid with the brightest future. I may be biased, but he really is the best.

But having had such a tough time as first-time parents, we're determined to have a different experience this time around. Unfortunately, as every parent of multiple offspring can attest, children don't come with rule books. And the how-to guide you wrote the first time around is a set of directions for a machine you no longer own. This new one needs different instructions altogether, and you get the joy of authoring the manual all over again. With the exception of the section titled "Eat, Poop, Change, Repeat," you still have a lot to figure out. And I swear, I feel just as tired and overwhelmed as last time.

But the difference?

This time, I know the sun is coming. And I know there's a special shade of green that can only be seen those first few weeks of a baby's life.

It comes when they fall asleep on your chest, cuddled in a ball with cheeks pressed into your chest and mouths agape, breathing ever so softly—because they trust that they're completely safe. It comes with that perfect scent that all newborns come wrapped in from the womb, instantly welcoming us adults into the magic of their existence when we lean in close enough to catch a whiff.

I wonder what the world would look like if we all got to breathe in some baby every morning?

And the green shines through every little coo, sigh, and cry—if you just know how to look for it. As if God in His infinite wisdom chose to find some small ways to brighten our days when He knows that, as the weariness sets in, it often brings with it a bit of despair.

Of loss of self, of freedom, of pants that fit.

Of changed expectations.

New babies tend to ruin plans for long days spent outside. They have a habit of increasing the stress and difficulty of almost any commute. They often require endless unloading of the diaper pail—thankfully, a chore that gets assigned to my husband. New babies can force you to sleep in the basement—an attempt to shield the rest of your family from their ceaseless crying. They seem to find a way of ruining almost every clean shirt you put on. And in my experience, they *always* make for a very cranky cooped-up toddler sibling and his sleep-deprived Mama.

But have you noticed that, as the rain comes pouring down, it magically unearths a color so vibrant it can almost offset the gray? It highlights the trees, the grass, the leaves in a shade of green that distracts from the wet. A heavenly attempt to try and liven up the mood. To remind us that with the rain comes life.

That without the rain, there would be no chance of green at all?

Rain, rain, go away—just not so fast I miss the green.

Naked and Afraid

The memory is vivid: I stood in front of the mirror, trying to figure out how to disguise the angry, seared skin not-so-cleverly hiding behind my patchy bangs. It was Junior High Picture Day, and in another pointless attempt at creating volume in my stick-straight hair, I'd scorched my forehead with my curling iron. A giant burn now stretched across my already acne-ridden skin.

Add in the sweater vest and the braces, and it's the garbage can for that yearbook.

Middle school really was the pits.

Fortunately for me, I have made a bit of progress in the beauty department since those challenging adolescent years. Unfortunately however, I never did figure out how to harness my locks with any type of perm, crimp, top knot, or wave. In spite of trying every mousse, hairspray, iron, and wand, my life's misfortune has been my stringy, curl-free hair hanging lifelessly in every photo ever taken of me.

Which explains my love for donning baseball hats and athletic headbands.

That is, until I delivered my second son, Levi Cross.

Along with the stretch marks that now line my formerly smooth abdomen, I've become the proud owner of an effortless beach wave.

Despite the fact that I rarely have time to plug in the blow dryer, my daily air-dried style trumps any former attempt at good Picture Day hair.

If only these waves could have showed up before high school.

As excited as I am to see my newfangled locks in all their wavy glory staring back at me in the mirror, I'm convinced they're just a small consolation prize meant to distract me from the incredibly ugly process my body has just endured.

For the second time.

My first pregnancy was no walk in the park. I got my first hemorrhoid and gained over thirty-five pounds. And after Micah finally made his debut, I noticed a number of underboob veins had showed up—unfortunately placed angry red lines that would permanently prevent my future as a bikini model.

But the second round of bringing forth life? For my little Levi love?

Have you heard of that show, *Naked and Afraid*?

Yeah, that's now the new title of my personal memoir.

Things happened to my body that were surely inspired by the devil himself. Towards the end of my pregnancy with him, I experienced what I called my daily knifings—stabbing pains smack dab in the middle of my lady parts—that would leave me sobbing on the kitchen floor. My doctor claimed my pubic bone had just begun to separate as a result of my extra large baby and quickly widening hips, but I'm pretty sure it was literal payback for being such a pain in the ass for so many years.

On top of that, when I stepped on the hospital scale the morning I went into labor, the three-digit sequence stating my weight blinked proof of my remarkable heft and provoked instant self-hatred. It was just an added bonus that my husband witnessed this neon curse of double hundred-weight flashing before us.

Awesome.

Then, when I left the hospital, my partially deflated stomach showed evidence of a multitude of subtle tears that had occurred in the muscular tissue of my six-pack of old, and the grooves left in their wake mocked my formerly fit self.

Pretty sure those puppies are gonna be there for the long haul.

Great.

And I won't even tell you about what's happening in my nether region today. Let's just say that I feel a little inside out when I run, jump, or attempt any physical intimacy with my husband. Try not to let yourself visualize that.

Whoops. Too late.

Here's to hoping some proper pelvic floor physical therapy can get us back in tip-top shape. If not, I get the privilege of having a bladder tuck when I grow up.

And this doesn't include the miscellaneous array of nausea, aches, and pains that plagued me for the entire nine months of my pregnancy and beyond.

Simply put, my body has been ravaged.

Horrified yet?

Yeah, me too.

If you're anything like me, losing control of your body can be incredibly difficult, especially if you've worked your whole life to keep it in shape. Historically, the feats I've asked my body to endure have usually left it stronger, thinner, and healthier—not scarred and maimed and hanging inside out in some unfortunate ways.

Becoming a mother has left my body more than a bit worse for wear, and it has been a struggle to come to terms with this new, injured version of myself. Ever wish you could disappear? That's how I felt when I finally admitted to my new fitness instructor the real reason I couldn't participate in some aspects of her boot camp class.

Rest in peace, jump rope. May we never dance again.

Just yesterday, I was driving home after picking Micah up from preschool. His cheeks were still flushed from his recent nap, and he was babbling about the soccer ball he'd kicked on the playground. Levi was snoozing in his car seat, and I could see his little belly rise and fall from the mirror secured on the back of his seat. A catchy new country song was playing on the radio, the windows were rolled down, and the sun was shining.

And for the briefest of moments, I felt like all was right in my little world. It was one of those rare chances you're given to feel your blessings in all of their fullness.

As we approached a stoplight, a beautiful brunette driving a silver SUV slowed to a stop next to us, and I realized her radio's tune matched ours. We looked across the lane and smiled at one another—both clearly enjoying the beautiful day. Upon a second glance in her direction, I caught sight of her beautiful wavy hair and her skinny tanned arms and her fresh coat of lip gloss. Her manicured hands tapped her steering wheel to the beat of the music.

I looked down and saw my muffin top bursting from the top of my old stained leggings.

Now normally, this beautiful girl would have struck envy into my heart. Her hair, her nails, her beautiful skin and her alleged freedom—all just a figment of my jealous imagination.

But this particular afternoon?

I felt sorry for her.

Sorry that she had an empty backseat. Pity that she was missing out on a two-year-old's rendition of telling a story about his day.

And just a touch sympathetic that she appeared to be wearing something far less comfortable than a pair of ancient, dirty stretch pants.

For once, I didn't make a mental list of everything I didn't have compared to her: a flat stomach or skinny arms or a chance to put on lip gloss. Instead I felt bad for what she was missing in her life when mirrored with the richness in mine. And in that instant, the gravity of all I've been given struck a healing chord in my soul.

Now, this woman could very well have two adorable kiddos that she was on her way to scoop up from their Nana's on her way home from the beauty salon, explaining away her current appearance. Or she could be completely joyful in her kidless freedom and the fact that she can sleep in any morning she wants.

We will never know. (Well, we may; it's a small town.)

But what I do know is that in that single moment, the Lord used this gorgeous girl to pierce through my ugly and gave answer to the personal sacrifice motherhood had demanded of me. It reminded me that although I may not look like I once did, I have more to look at in my rearview mirror than any one heart could hope. In that instant, He brought forth a picture of what I might look like without my children, and it wasn't nearly as beautiful as I remembered.

And hey, at least I have great hair. And let's be honest, I've always been wearing yoga pants.

Summer

Records

I stand in the shower and cry hot, shameful tears. Tears of rage. Tears of regret. Tears of utter exhaustion.

So many tears.

It's been a week for the record books. Record number of tantrums from my two-and-change-year-old. Record number of wake-ups in the middle of the night from my four-month-old (sleep regressions are REAL in our house, y'all). Record number of losing-my-freaking-mind moments, rich with a yelling Mama, attacked kids, and zero winners.

As the piping hot water pounds my back and runs down the sides of my face, my body shakes as I let go of every shred of emotion I have left. With matted hair clinging to my blotchy cheeks, I hang my head and the flood of memories—a highlight reel of my failures—drowns me.

There was the incident at Aldi over the veggie straws. The episode where a very disappointed toddler learned that the farm we were visiting didn't open for three more hours. There was the peeing on the floor (twice!) at the library—a special double whammy of mortification and soggy paper towels.

There was the expensive art class and the attention span that only lasted five minutes. The full-body wipe-out when Micah took off in a foot race across a tile floor while outfitted in Crocs. The pacifying with donuts.

And the subsequent sugar high and crash. In the middle of Target.

The cashier actually said out loud, "You seem to be having one of those days."

To which I replied, "Welcome to my every day!"

In my opinion, teenagers who still have their figures, the freedom to apply mascara in the morning, and no need for under-eye cream should know better than to make comments to frazzled mothers with their hands full who are just trying their best to get through the freaking day.

She should have known; she works at Target. It's the mecca for frazzled mothers with their hands full who are just trying their best to get through the freaking day.

For the record.

After all, it's been a week for the records.

There was the running away from me in the parking lot. The puking on my only clean shirt. The blow-out in the car seat at church. The refusing of the chicken nuggets that had been cooked on request. The plans with girlfriends cancelled due to a cranky baby, a late departure, and traffic.

Earlier this week, as my son threw to the floor every single godforsaken piece of rice that had once been on his plate, I actually just hung my head in my hands in the middle of a Chipotle. Elbows up on the dirty metal table before me, I bowed and tried to shut it all out—all my failed mothering, all his defiant behavior, all the looks from all the people around me.

It didn't work.

I just took a deep breath, grabbed the wipes, did my best with cleaning the floor, and tried not to let his insistence on hopping out of the restaurant like a frog—all while screaming *RIBBIT*—bother me while I hauled his brother, a car seat, a diaper bag, our leftovers, two water bottles, and a shred of my dignity to the car.

And all on no wine. Dang baby weight and an overdue attempt at the Whole30. Why did I think this month was the time to introduce some self-restraint?

I tell you. The record books.

And the tears.

But before long, I hear a cry from the baby monitor, breaking through the rushing water (and the self-pity).

So I look up. Wipe my face. Turn off the water. Step out.

And start over.

Leaving the failures on the floor of my shower.

Summer

Again, Again

*I*n complete surrender to the suburbs—and contributing to the quickly fleeting sense that we'll ever live a sexy lifestyle again—this summer, we purchased a family season pass to Six Flags Great America. I'm only slightly embarrassed to admit how excited this purchase has made me.

We may or may not go every week.

Blessed with a two-year-old monster child who towers over many of his friends twice his age, Micah's off-the-charts height qualifies him to ride quite a few adult rides—including an entry-level roller coaster called the Whizzer, quick to become his greatest obsession.

I'm a very proud mama to this fearless little boy.

But every dang time we get to the amusement park, we're forced to engage in a battle of the ages. Our son's lack of patience—in direct conflict with his deep desire to ride this coaster "again, again, again" and in combination with his inability to understand what it means to wait his turn—means he's regularly having an epic-level breakdown while waiting to board this ride.

Why did we ever let him go on this thing in the first place?

And why can't these amusement park employees figure out a more efficient system for boarding and deboarding? Something about a screaming toddler makes time stop in its tracks.

"Just a few more minutes, buddy."

"It's almost our turn."

"Can you count how many people are still in front of us?"

"Are you sure you don't want to just go ride something else?"

"Are you just committed to making this as hard as possible for both of us?"

"Show me how you can take a couple deep breaths."

"No, you can't climb over that railing."

"Your dad is taking you next time."

"Almost there!"

And finally, it's our turn.

"Oh, thank you, sweet Jesus."

Once he's aboard, the joy on my child's face is instant and unmatched. He throws both his hands in the air while laughing the entire two minutes we wind around the track. And, I've got to be honest with you, it's a decent little roller coaster!

I wonder when was the last time I loved anything as much as Micah loves riding the Whizzer?

Joy like that is worth the wait.

But as soon as we pull into the station, he cries, *"Again! Again!"*

And I have to explain again, again—while physically dragging his giant body out of the car—that we have to go wait in line again, again before we get to ride the coaster again, again.

Cue the alligator tears.

Cue the people staring at us.

And cue the sweating mother. (My body always responds to embarrassing situations by doing the most embarrassing thing it can—pitting out my t-shirt and drawing a sweat mustache.)

"Oh, the things we do for our children," I say to myself as we climb down the stairs and find ourselves at the back of a too-long line again, again.

"Seriously, where is your father?"

Sitting on a shaded bench reading his phone with a sleeping baby in the stroller next to him.

Good. Ness.

Teaching my strong-willed young child how to wait his turn has to be harder than just about anything. It's a maddening process of corralling a stubborn little egocentric, amazing human who wants what he wants, right this second, immediately, and without a care in the world for how his whining, crying, tantrumy body looks to anyone around him. The list of places my son has thrown his body on the ground in reckless protest is exhaustive. Just ask the other Moms whose children seem to have a rational response to hearing the word "no"—I'm certain that a certain unruly toddler and his underskilled, impatient mama will be the talk of their next play date.

But the reckless passion that can lead to Micah throwing himself on the floor of a play place when I tell him he can't have macaroni and cheese at 10:30 in the morning?

Limitless.

It's the same fearlessness that allows the kid to ditch the fork and pick up a slice of birthday cake with his two grubby hands and shove it directly in his face—the most efficient method he can derive to get that goodness into his mouth.

It's the same fearlessness that allows him the freedom to dance in a room full of strangers when his favorite song begins to play. And it's the source of his willingness to forgo putting on pants so he can run into the room to show everyone his penis.

Yes, I just said penis.

It's probably one of Micah's current favorite words.

"What's that, Mommy?" he asks as he tugs on his scrotum.

"It's your scrotum, honey. Please don't say that to your friends or teachers," I plead.

"SCWOTUM! SCWOTUM! SCWOTUM!"

I told you. Monster child.

Public displays of "scwotums" aside, one of the unexpected gifts of parenting is that my children are teaching me just as often as I'm attempting to teach them. In this case, my two-year-old has been challenging me to claim my own desires—and the emotions to go with them—in reckless abandon.

To be willing to own my truth, no matter the audience.

To just go for it.

Whatever it is.

I wish I wasn't so concerned with the perception of others. I wish I could be free from the weight of my insecurities—free from the script I've written for myself over the years. But just like my toddler, learning these boundaries will be an ongoing learning process.

As Micah's uninhibited way of living comes in contact with my overly buttoned-up version—and my patience, on the daily—I hope he'll continue to challenge me to recapture a bit of my original self. The fiery and spirited little girl my mother reminisces about who'd never met a stranger, performed self-written plays for the whole neighborhood out of our garage, and started her own landscaping business with a Red Flyer full of pinecones.

I'd love to recapture her bravery—and her profit margins.

In this process of shepherding a little man's spirit, I hope I don't squash his. Instead, I pray I can continue to let his spirit—his bravery—teach me. If I'm lucky, I'll become a bit more like her again.

Again.

End of Summer

Incapable

I lie on the couch trying to catch a quick snooze before the baby awakes from his morning crap nap, when a text from my best friend chimes on the table next to me.

"I looked in the mirror this morning and was appalled at how haggard and old I look. I just feel like I'm failing in every aspect of my life right now—as a wife, mother, sister, daughter, and friend. I feel burned out and generally incapable. And I hate that, because both boys are at such cute, fun ages, and I feel like I'm not appreciating it fully. I'm taking all the practical steps I can think of, but until I'm getting sleep, I don't know if anything will make much difference. Sleep deprivation is seriously torture. I can't handle it! Remind me of this when I say I want another baby someday!"

She put my exact feelings into the exact right words.

Like her, my kids aren't sleeping either. Hence, the mid-morning nap attempt. I, too, am appalled at how haggard I look when I catch a glimpse of my tired face in the mirror. And you should see the acne ravaging my skin since weaning Levi. But vanity aside, what strikes the loudest chord in her message is her feeling of failure. The sense of burnout. Of falling short. Of being incapable.

Incapable.

That word *incapable* rolls around in my mind for days.

Since our boys arrived on the scene, I've confessed to my husband countless times that I must not be cut out for this whole motherhood thing. That I must be missing some secret sauce that both of our amazing mothers (as well as that really peppy, super-on-top-of-it and I-just-love-being-a-mom neighbor woman) possesses.

Maybe I'm just incapable of doing this job well?

But you know what's funny? My dear, texting friend is one of the women I so often consider a natural, amazing mother—one who sets the bar for motherhood and against whom I don't even come close to measuring.

When I watch her mother her children, I am in awe at her grace. I see her gentle spirit and her patience and her commitment to her boys' wellbeing above all else. I witness her sacrifice her sleep and her career and her wants daily. In all she does, she puts her husband and kids before herself. Meanwhile, I struggle in all of the above and recently moved my seven-month-old to formula for purely selfish reasons.

Best yet, I'm privileged to know the two sweet boys she's raising. And they exude the joy she invests into their little lives.

Yet somehow, when she looks in the mirror, all she sees is a haggard face and her failures staring back at her? There's something deeply wrong with that picture. Perhaps what we mothers are most incapable of seeing clearly is our own reflections. Somehow, our perceived flaws mask the beauty in the hard, and we remain unable to see just how capable we are of this calling to raise our families.

In therapy a million years ago, I got frustrated with my paid-best-friend's unwillingness to tell me how to handle a difficult situation with my family. I wanted her to give me the quick fix, the right answer. Instead, she said her job was to hold up the mirror for me, to tell me what she saw in my reflection and to allow me to work out the steps to go from there.

Looking back, I'm grateful she didn't rob me of the chance to learn I was capable of handling something hard. From that tricky situation, I found that I could communicate my feelings and navigate conflict with people I love on my own, like an adult. And turns out, it was a positive experience for everyone.

I'm glad she held up the mirror and showed me just how capable I was.

So often I find myself feeling grateful for a friend that trusts me with her reflection, albeit the flawed version she saw that morning. Not only do I find comfort in the fact that I'm not the only one feeling like such a failure in this season, I get to recognize that what we feel and what we are can be dramatically different things.

So my job is to remind her of the truth.

Where she sees failure, I see fierce love. Where she sees haggard, I see beauty in the sacrifice. Where she feels discouraged, I declare her holy call of mother and wife.

Where she sees incapable, I refuse to let her believe it.

Sometimes we just need someone else to hold up the mirror and tell us what's really staring back at us.

Early Fall

Framed

Mothers never choose pictures of themselves for their Christmas cards. Have you noticed that?

A friend of mine is a professional photographer who specializes in family portraits and newborn baby photo sessions. As her two daughters got a little more independent, she gradually invested in her passion for photography and grew a healthy business by leveraging her picture-taking skills with her ability to successfully corral and engage young children to create a false—and beautiful—sense of calm in the prints she makes.

Family holiday shoots are her bread and butter.

Session after session and gallery after gallery, she takes note of the images selected for printing and mailing, a job most frequently assigned to the mother: Husband; Kids; Maybe a shot of Mom in profile, or from the shoulders up or draped in her children.

A mother's warped self-image impacting the actual images chosen to showcase her family.

We all know that family Christmas pictures are a disaster to take. This year, both of my kids are screaming as we load the car. Micah's shoes are "ouchy," Levi's sweater is way too big, and I can't find a lip color.

Of course, Dan looks perfect, but he's annoying like that.

The temperature has dropped to a level where a responsible

parent would have packed coats. On top of that, it's a total windstorm at the park where we meet our photographer, so curling my hair for the second time this year was a total waste of time.

We do our best to salvage a crap morning—bribing the toddler with snacks and wrapping the baby in a blanket to keep him from getting frostbite. Our photographer ensures us that he's gotten some great shots.

I'm not convinced.

A couple weeks later when the online gallery hits our inboxes, I text Dan:

Well, not our best year for family photos, eh?

His response:

Really? I thought they turned out great!

While I lament the lack of decent options for our Christmas card—my face looking swollen, my hair blowing sideways in the wind, my post-baby belly bursting out of my "big" jeans, my colorless smile—my husband just sees the people he loves most in the world smiling in matching outfits with autumn leaves bursting in the background.

"Pick any of them! I loved them all," he says.

I hold my breath as I click "purchase" for a hundred cards I hate.

And since I paid extra to have them stamped and mailed out this year, our card arrives before most on our mailing list carve their turkey, an oversight that ensures everyone will stare at my puffy face for weeks on end without any neighboring cards to buffer the blow.

"Beautiful family."

"Love your card!"

"First one here!"

Yet, all I've been able to think about is what I'll do differently next year. And I will have lip color, dang it!

There is more than one issue at play here: not only am I far too concerned with appearances, but I could do with a little lesson in self-love.

Because as I line our back door with the cards we've received, I notice my photographer friend is right—very few mothers are at the center of the portraits chosen for the family Christmas mailer.

Sure, they can be found. In the witty words written, in the perfectly coordinated outfits, the picture-perfect setting, and the timely arrival of the cards themselves. Maybe you'll spot them on the back, but not often enough on the front.

Where have we gone?

Learning from experience, my friend now asks her clients to have the husband select his favorite photos first. Startled, women usually ask why. And she responds, "Let someone who loves you pick the images first."

What she's found is that, in his favorite image, usually his wife stands smack dab in the center, kids gazing up at her, with him proudly off to the side looking at the glory she's created for him. After all, she's the center of their world. The force of love, the glue, the heart of their family. And that's where the beauty begins.

If only we would believe it.

Fall

In Sickness

All I know is that everything hurts: my throat, my head, my body. I wake up in a full-body sweat from a 102-degree fever, and my over-the-counter meds are not proving worthy of the task at hand.

On a mission to feel better, I leave the kids with my husband and trudge through the drugstore in my crusty pajamas, filling up a basket with cold meds, Gatorade, and popsicles before heading back to bed.

Sadly, my purchases prove as pointless as my immune system in the war taking place in my upper respiratory system.

Three full days later and I'm barely on the mend. In that time, Dan has moved to the guest room, the kids have been kept away, and I watch *The Office* reruns—not even the good seasons—on my laptop while drinking my weight in sugary electrolyte drinks and nibbling on saltines. I make sure not to miss a dose of Ibuprofen.

It's pretty darn awful.

Terrified of ruining the approaching holiday with sick babes, I live my life in a full quarantine and Dan's tasked with ninety-nine percent of the parenting responsibilities. As Monday becomes Friday at a glacial pace, I realize I haven't spent this much time by myself in years. And for this restful break, I just have to pay the small price of enduring the world's worst "cold."

Doesn't seem fair.

I can't tell you how many times I've fantasized about a dark, kid-free night's sleep. I've dreamt about having our king-sized bed all to myself so I wouldn't have to deal with my husband's heavy breathing interrupting my ability to fall asleep. I've envied those friends that can sleep in on a Saturday without interruption. And I always love a good excuse to binge-watch my favorite sitcoms—including the bad seasons.

Yet, as these dreams are realized, roped off in our master bedroom I find myself feeling only one thing: lonely.

I miss my family more than my health.

I've heard it said that when you have children, a piece of your heart lives outside of your body, walking around. After my illness-imposed isolation, a fuller truth is realized: your kids aren't just a piece of you, a part of your heart; your children are a part of who you have become. I have multiplied. Or I have divided. I'm not sure of the math, but I know that without those two little boys in my life, I am not whole.

And my husband and I have been one since we said our vows—*in sickness and in health, until death do us part.*

So as I bury my head in the covers and contemplate whether Pam should have just let Jim take the job in Philadelphia or if Erin could be Phyllis's biological daughter, I also take a few moments to let my missing out sink in, knowing that there will soon be a time when I will again covet an opportunity to be alone with my thoughts and my reruns.

My thoughts keep circling back to my new truth: I am no longer the person I was before Dan, before Micah, before Levi. I am so much more. Or less.

Those three sum up my life.

When my symptoms wane and I can safely cradle my babies without fear of infecting them, I'm thrilled to shower them with a weeks' worth of love and affection. And, as these things go, I'm pretty sure it only takes one morning of dealing with a cranky, teething baby and a strong-willed toddler for me to lament my new lease on life.

Oh, the irony of motherhood at its finest.

And because all things are best said by Michael Scott from *The Office*, I leave you with this:

"I love babies. I think they are beautiful in all sorts of different ways. I try to pick up and hold a baby every day, if possible, because it nourishes me. It feeds my soul. Babies are drawn to me. And I think it's because they see me as one of them. But cooler and with my life put together a little bit more."

Yes, Michael, they really are a special kind of soul-nourishing magic.

Fall

Daughter

Commuting to the suburbs for an apple-picking adventure brought Colleen to my neck of the woods for the first time since we moved north. I jump at the chance for us to spend the morning together.

As she unloads her car, and carts her kids in, I turn on the coffee. With the boys anxious to play—*read: fight over*—trains and trucks, we cross our legs on my freshly-carpeted basement floor, cradle our steaming mugs and attempt to squeeze six months of life updates into one short visit. With four little boys between us—the youngest two fresh to our families and still nursing on our laps—life has gotten in the way of our friendship, as it often has a habit of doing.

But seeing her still feels like letting out a giant sigh of relief.

She married one of my long-time good friends in the city, and in a gracious way that's not always guaranteed, she chose to accept me with open arms into her circle of loved ones. Entering motherhood in tandem—and both choosing to leave our corporate careers on the back burner in response—there were many mornings during that first year with the first round of boys that we linked arms and pushed strollers down city sidewalks, waiting for our husbands—and our bangin' pre-baby bodies—to come home.

That is, until a second pregnancy caused Dan and me to finally cave and buy the house in the suburbs. With the play set. And the finished basement. And the picket—well, wrought iron—fence.

And all of sudden, without much notice, my nicely manicured suburban sidewalks were about an hour from the hustle and bustle of her city streets—and nobody's got time for that commute with two babes in the back seat.

So spring turned into summer, and summer turned into fall. And newborns turned into babies, and babies turned into toddlers.

And our friendship was left on that back burner, along with those corporate careers.

But as the first hint of fall color begins to make its move on the edges of the trees, the chance to escape the urban jungle for the suburban orchards has presented a chance for us to catch up in fast-motion—regularly being interrupted for potty breaks and nursing breaks and snack breaks, of course. And as familiar friends often do, we circle back to a well-worn topic between us: our sticky relationship with our careers, or lack thereof.

And as she shares that she finally walked into a counseling office to work out some of her anxiety around leaving her kids in daycare two days a week so she can financially contribute to her family at a job she hates and has been juggling for the past year, I let out a breath I didn't realize I'd been holding.

And have been holding for months.

And as I confess my Mom guilt about putting Micah in daily Montessori so that I can write a book that still remains a little more dream than reality, and certainly does little for our family's bottom line, she nods in judgment-free support.

She explains that with the help of her counselor, she's realized that as she tries to figure out what she is meant to do in regards to her job, her family, her finances, she's really just facing off with one topic: *her identity as a daughter of God.*

And is that identity enough for her?

• • • • • • • • • • •

I still remember the first time I used the word "son" in reference to my very own living and breathing human being. We'd just returned from the hospital (and all of that birthing business), and we had a fresh-faced baby in tow—expertly strapped into our overpriced car seat by the kindly nursing staff. My own mother had flown in for the occasion, of course, and my first official job as a parent was to put a call in to the pediatrician to make my baby's first post-delivery appointment.

And as the receptionist picked up, I found myself saying, "Hi there. I'd like to make an appointment with doctor so-and-so for my son, Micah." And I caught myself.

I had a son.

Holy goodness, I had a son.

A SON.

What an odd thing to say out loud.

After I hung up, I turned to Mom and she read my mind, as she has a habit of doing. "Did it feel weird to say it out loud?" she asked.

"YES."

And the gravity of my new identity started to sink in.

I had a son.

I was a mother.

Holy goodness, I WAS A MOTHER.

Who went off and let me become a mother?

My new job responsibilities increased—the diapers, the feeding schedule, the never-ending laundry—but I found that my own identity—my own sense of person—diminished in tandem. Who was I outside of my child? Did my life have more meaning than just keeping him alive and well and loved?

Somewhere along the way, I found myself in possession of two kids, but I'd gotten more than a little lost among them. When I became a mother, in many ways, I forgot who I was. I forgot that I was first a child.

I forgot that I was first a *daughter*. No, *I am* the daughter of the One True Living and Holy King.

Yes, I am a child of God.

And if there's one thing that becoming a mother has taught me, it is that your child is your child is your child. There's absolutely nothing that your child can do to change that identity.

It is permanent.

Your child is loved. Your child is known. Your child is yours, and your heart yearns for them to stand tall in that knowledge.

I will always be a child—a daughter—of God.

So in the midst of loving my children, I'm working on remembering that fact.

Reminding myself that I am loved.

Hard stop.

I am known.

Full stop.

I am a child of God.

And He wants me to stand tall in that knowledge.

•••••••••••

Our time together goes too fast, as it has a habit of doing with familiar friends. But after we hug and wave our goodbyes, I'm left with a portion of our conversation on repeat for days to come.

Is my identity as a daughter of God enough?

And I realize that it really doesn't feel like it.

Both of us earned our college degrees, moved to Chicago, and started the infamous climb up a pair of nice corporate ladders, each landing at a rung that paid us reasonably well to put those degrees to good use. For years, we woke up faithfully each Monday morning to an alarm that told us to get up, to get back on the ladder, to keep climbing, to answer the emails, to show up with the pitch prepared, to process the invoice, to do the work.

Where the heck had we been climbing to?

I'm not sure I ever knew.

As children came, notices were given and business cards were exchanged for diaper bags. High heels were replaced with running shoes and blazers were traded for hoodies.

But in our run out the door to answer the worthy call of motherhood, we left something behind in those office buildings: pieces of our story, parts of ourselves, and identities that had taken shape over years of climbing.

And let's not forget those really nice second paychecks.

What we're both realizing, with the help of familiar friends, faithful professional counselors, and caring spouses, is that it's okay if the quick shift in job title to MOM didn't come easily. It's not that we're bad at the role or need to make changes (or need to avoid making changes).

Life is going to be a process of making choices and living with their impact. But if we don't remember that we're daughters first, will we ever be content in making them?

Probably not.

So in my inability to figure my life out for myself, in my own indecision, with the help of a dear friend, I'm starting back at the beginning. I'm waking up in the morning, looking at myself in the mirror and reminding myself of the only truth that matters:

I am a daughter of God.

I am a daughter of God.

I am a daughter of God.

I am a daughter.

And also a mother.

I have a purpose.

Even when I can't see it.

I am enough.

For my kids and for myself.

I am loved.

And I can choose to love myself, too.

I was made for something great.

Even if it's going to take a while to figure out.

It's been a rocky process to reach this new level of self-acceptance. My identity has been broken and reshaped through motherhood— and it's been so much harder than I expected. But because I'm a daughter of God, I must claim the complete freedom I've been given. Freedom to live without fear. Freedom to love and to be loved. And freedom to fail. So in my freedom, I walk forward in faith.

And most days, I have no flipping idea where I'm going. But I am a daughter of God. I choose for that to be enough.

PART FOUR: OWNING IT

Holy Work

*D*an gave me the afternoon off for some much-needed self-care, so I run to the nail salon at lightning speed—my feet are DUE.

As the massage chair does its best to pummel my tired body into a state of relaxation, I overhear the conversation of two women next to me—both with teenage kids at the beginning of their freshman year of college. They're laughing because one of them had just overnighted a new iPhone to her son after his "screen cracked when he dropped it while climbing into his bunk bed in his dorm room."

Riiiiiight.

We all know that a few choice details were intentionally left out when he emailed his Mom in a screen-disabled panic.

"When are they going to realize just how much we do for them?" she laments.

"I bet they'll say thank you when they're in their twenties," her friend replies.

And because I've never been known to keep my mouth shut in these types of not-so-private sharing situations, I chime in, "When they're blessed with babies of their own. I never knew just how much my mother did for me—or how deeply she loved me—until I had my boys."

"How old are your babies?" she inquires with a knowing smile.

"Two-and-a-half and a half."

Her eyes mist slightly. "It really does happen as fast as they say it does. Hold them close."

This isn't the only time one of my more seasoned sisters has encouraged me to soak in these moments with my young children. And I don't know if my hormones are going for one of their famous rides or if God is using these little interactions to soften my soul, but every time I hear this type of reminder, I grieve just a little for how fast the clock turns for my little family.

Which makes me feel a lot better about the many other moments I find myself grieving the other parts of me that died a quick death when I became a Mom: my sales career, my social life after 9 PM, and my desire to impact the world, to name a few. Sometimes the list of things I've lost seems so much longer than the list of what I've gained. In these moments of mourning, I grieve the woman who knew just how her days mattered.

I volunteered with kids. I sang at church. I blogged. I travelled. I made my own money. I gave too little of it away.

I had a heart for others. I had time to have a heart for others. I wanted to change the world. I even knew what the heck was going on in the world.

My days mattered and I knew it.

These days, I feel like the menial tasks that demand my attention—most of which revolve solely around my children and our household—are pretty insignificant.

I change diapers. I make dinner. I manage preschool drop-off. I plan play dates. I buy more paper towels and new jammies and an orange shirt for the Halloween party, just in the nick of time.

And once in a while, I drink my coffee hot.

Most of these acts, these sacrifices for my kids, are thankless. And according to my new pedicuring friends, they'll remain so for a good long while.

So it can be hard to see how I matter.

Not too long ago, when I was scrolling into the black internet hole of a middle-of-the-night breastfeeding session, I stumbled across a video of these innovators who created edible water pods using some sort of brown seaweed. If you're not in the know like yours truly, let me describe these tiny world-changing creations to you: basically, imagine one of those water-based Chinese finger traps of your youth, but delete the part where you stick in your grubby fingers, and shrink it down to a bite-sized blob. These little bubbles of hydration can be easily stored and popped into your mouth whenever thirst strikes—ideally replacing our population's gross dependence on single-use plastic water bottles, of which fifty billion are made annually.

So, world-changing? I would say so.

And here I thought boxed water was crazy.

Baby milked, I flopped back into bed and found myself wishing that I could have the time and/or skills to dream up something as amazing as water pods. That my life could so positively impact the world as to eliminate a whole bunch of nasty planet-killing plastic.

Or at least have the headspace to dream up something cool like boxed water. *

That my life could really matter.

Now this may seem like a strange moment of epiphany, but I'm not the One who writes the script upstairs. All I know is that, in my heart I heard, "Your work is holy work, too."

I'm a part of a group at my church called MOPS: Mothers of Preschoolers. It's an excuse to spend a couple of childless hours a month with other women and a chance to drink that hot coffee I like so much. At our chapter, we eat a lavish breakfast and do cool crafts. And despite my lack of skills in the craft department, I've managed to make some really great friends who are living out a similar version of life where their kids eat up most of their time and brain power. The icing on this kids-in-free-childcare cake is that they assign each group a mentor mom—envision a knowledgeable grandma with a huge heart—to proffer her very welcome parenting and hot glue gun advice.

At our first meeting, our mentor mom, Monica, shared the one thing she wished she could tell her younger self, if she were in our tired shoes. You know what she said?

"I wish I could tell my younger self that the work of motherhood is holy work."

What she said didn't really sink in until that quiet voice cut through the night and quieted my comparing:

Your work is holy work, too.

Who knows? Maybe Micah or Levi will become the inventor of the next iteration of human hydration, saving the planet and many lives in one fell swoop. Or maybe they'll just be kind. Either way, mothering the two of them with my whole self matters—regardless of the rest of the details. It may at times feel thankless or meaningless or maddening or just plain boring, but it is holy.

After all, it lasts a lifetime.

I hope I can begin to proclaim my motherhood for its holiness, not its holes.

One time in college, my best friend and I dreamed up a million-dollar idea called the Bod Pod. The Bod Pod was a sports bra that could both carry and support the hefty weight of an ancient first-generation iPod. It would come in a range of colors, would waterproof your music device from your sweat session, and be affordable to a woman on a college budget. Unfortunately, not long afterward, Nike came out with a perfectly pocketed version of their best-selling boob gear. Alas, opportunity for fame and fortune was lost just as quickly as it'd come.

A New Year

A Great Adventure

Parenthood has not been kind to our marriage.

As we planned our wedding—choosing flowers, ordering invitations, tasting cake—we were inundated with friendly warnings that we should expect our first year as husband and wife to be a doozy. Sitting across the desk from our pastor, we were counseled to prepare for new conflicts, a season fraught with the challenges of adjusting to permanent life together.

And that first year?

One of the best of my life.

It can't hurt that we gallivanted Chicago with amazing friends, attended a church that filled us to the brim, and when that got boring, traded our nine-to-fives for one-way tickets to Europe and embarked on the five-month backpacking journey of a lifetime.

So, fraught with challenges?

The only challenge I recall was deciding what country we were headed to next. Times were tough.

When we landed stateside—exciting social life intact—we walked into the next chapter of our story—parenthood—with the expectation of continuing our great adventure together with similar ease and grace.

As we prepared for our son's arrival—choosing a name, picking out a stroller, washing tiny baby clothes—we were flooded with congratulations and told to expect the arrival of our child to be the most amazing thing to ever happen to us. During my baby shower, our closest friends and family shared their well-wishes for our growing family, anticipation for the sweet season to come.

And that first year?

One of the hardest of my life.

It certainly didn't help that most of our friends were still out gallivanting, childless and carefree, or that we attended a church without air conditioning, making it a near impossibility to bring along a fresh baby, or that my new nine-to-five had transformed into a 24/7 with no reprieve or passport stamp in sight.

So, the most amazing thing to ever happen to our marriage?

All I can recall is that we had a colicky baby in a poorly built condo and a union we didn't recognize or much care for.

And it's turned into almost three years fraught with challenges.

Don't get me wrong, there have been countless beautiful moments, too, but we can both agree that this version of our partnership is not what we expected, nor the one we want to live in forever.

Yesterday, we spent the majority of the day in one of those ongoing arguments that began over nothing and became something that had been there for a long time, taking new shape over naptime and reaching crescendo after putting the kids to bed.

Me in tears. Him emotionally checking out. Both of us frustrated.

Miserable.

Tired.

Needing change, breakthrough, SOMETHING.

We hit the pillow, worn out and unresolved, my least favorite way to go to bed.

Yet this morning I return from the gym to find that my husband has made me coffee—the familiar smell hitting my nose the moment I walk in the door. Bless his tea-drinking heart, but even with a quarter cup of cream, it's the color of dirt and tastes like it, too.

And as I dump my still-full mug on the driveway of the drive-thru and trade that cup of tar for an easy, easy hot cup of joe, I thank God for a husband who's the first to wave the white flag—even if he doesn't know his way around the new coffee machine he gave me for Christmas.

With a reminder of his love for me warm in my hand, I reflect on the conflict that has plagued our relationship lately, and realize that one theme has surfaced through the muck: neither one of us has come to terms with our new identity since having children.

And our marriage has become the casualty of this identity crisis.

As a mother, I've wrestled with my decision to stay at home and raise my kids, a commitment that's felt more like a cage than a blessing. Both Dan and I were raised by amazing stay-at-home mothers who were the picture of love and stability in our childhoods and serve as the standard for the family dynamic we've been striving for. A full-time, stay-at-home mom is the ideal we created—and have stubbornly stuck to—since we first learned children were on their way.

And I'm miserable.

I've become increasingly unhappy, longing for something different out of my days and riddled with guilt for feeling that way. Still, I keep questioning the cost to my family should I make a different choice.

Now, I haven't regretted one moment of being with my children, but there's a part of my soul I've spent three years quieting with force—a part of me begging to be named and honored, but instead bubbling out as anger and resentment towards my husband and his alleged male-given freedom.

My discontent with my own status has been a root cause for many a challenge in our relationship.

Meanwhile, Dan has been on a particularly painful journey of his own. He closed down his business after a decade of success, he pursued a secondary degree that may not pay off in the way he expected, and he struggles to balance the emotional needs of his dissatisfied wife and his commitment to his kids and the heavy burden of providing for our family.

His discontent with his current status has been a root cause for many a challenge in our relationship.

In the midst of this season of instability in our marriage, we've been blessed with the two most amazing, healthy little boys whose souls are rooted in actual joy—two little people who've given our lives so much more purpose and love than we see when we're focused on our own discontent. When we take the time to look at our life correctly, we have hearts filled with awe and gratitude, yet when our own identities are threatened, we're back on the struggle bus.

Both with ourselves and each other.

Ironically, this week marks the beginning of a new year, a natural time for reflection, goal setting, hope. When I look back on the past year clearly—with a heart filled with awe and gratitude—I'm able to see how good it was to us: we welcomed another healthy son into our family, we bought our first home, we moved nearer to our family, and we celebrated Dan finishing grad school after two and a half years of really hard work. But on the days where we argue for hours on end about the same old issues—with no tangible progress toward solving them—it's hard not to feel like our whole year was a loss.

As my husband likes to say, the human capacity for being miserable can prove endless.

Turning to a fresh page in the calendar, I'm hopeful we can start to see our lives with more clarity. I refuse to continue to live in this muck, allowing our individual identity issues to rob us of the marriage we desire, and keeping us from savoring this precious season with our young children. Now that the root has been revealed, it's time to address it. This new year will require us to get uncomfortable, to make some changes, some tough decisions. We may not get them all right, but it's time to turn the corner.

It's time to decide that we can be different.

That might mean I don't stay home full-time. That might mean my husband gets a new job. That might mean we put our own needs on the front burner in order to better care for our marriage and our family.

So far parenthood has not been kind to our marriage, but I refuse to believe that we're incapable of change. We're still showing up. He's still making bad coffee. And I'm still pretending to drink it.

My prayer is that we can start wrestling with the Lord for these decisions, instead of with each other. I'm confident He can handle it better than we can. The marriage we want depends on it. The healthy family we want to give our boys depends on it.

Our future depends on it.

Dan and I have visited over twenty countries together, all but one before we had our boys. He'd always say that we were on a Great Adventure together. Well, somewhere along the way, we lost our map and ourselves. We stopped writing our story. We stopped looking forward to the next stop on our journey together.

Somewhere along the way, we just stopped.

So this is the year we choose to begin our new Great Adventure.

The one where we go somewhere new—together. The one where we each find a route that will lead to our own fulfillment, even if it requires a big change in direction. The one where we see our lives clearly, creating space for more awe and gratitude.

I have a feeling it will be our Greatest Adventure yet—it's the one where we have a family to bring along.

New Year's Day

Owning It

Michaja and Travis, two of our dearest friends, have been hosting a New Year's Day gathering at their condo in the city for many years—since long before children were added to the guest list. Our circle fondly calls it "Best Day Ever" and we commune over the world's most unhealthy dips and desserts, drinking more champagne than we did the night before—and all in the comfort of our sweatpants. In a collective boycott of Uber's surge pricing and crowded bars with bad drink specials the night before, year after year, our group gathers in the comfort that comes with the daylight.

And we laugh—sometimes a bit tipsy—all day long.

This year is the first time we're forced to drive rather than walk, our suburban relocation making us the out-of-towners of the crew. Lugging in our two young boys—and all the gear they require for a long day of celebrating: the diaper bag, the pack-and-play, the many snacks—I second-guess our decision to sign up for the extra work this day of fun will require.

Yet as I sit on the carpeted floor upstairs with some of my favorite women in the world, wearing yoga pants and sipping Prosecco from a plastic cup, watching a gaggle of young kids crawling and playing between us, I inhale our new version of a new year. Drinking in the beauty—and chaos—of it all.

Thankful for forever friendships that are strong enough to withstand the test of life change.

On the dizzy drive home—appreciating a husband who's not

much of a drinker—I think about how it's been challenging to be one of the first of our friends to forge new paths in life, especially when they lead you away from women you've been standing alongside for years. I'm ever so grateful for a circle of faithful sisters that have stood by me—and, later, us—for over a decade. Yet when I moved forward with the marriage, and the babies, and the house in the suburbs, my choices brought change to my life to which my closest girlfriends could not relate.

My friend Michaja has been the one exception. She and Trav were married three weeks before us, she delivered her first son, Crosby, a few weeks before Micah, and delivered her second son, Wells, a couple of months after Levi.

By God's grace, our lives have grown forward in tandem for over twelve years.

I like to think God knew these new roads in life would be challenging for me to walk alone, so He provided a trusted friend—someone who's known me through it all—with whom to navigate the new waters of wife life and motherhood. Together, she and I are learning to straddle our two worlds: our circle of fierce, amazing girlfriends and our growing young families.

Yet sometimes having a companion walking next to you can force comparisons. While I've been on the struggle bus for these big transitions, especially motherhood, I've watched in awe at how easily she seems to be able to marry her many identities—able to be an amazing mom, supportive wife, and invested friend—with ease. On top of that, she's also a successful business owner and working parent.

If I'm being honest, there have been moments when being witness to her graceful transitions—in light of my regular stumbling—has caused me to feel like a failure. Yet if I look a bit more closely at her life—how she makes her decisions and approaches each new phase—the reason she makes it all look so effortless is being revealed.

The one thing she does that I so often do not?

She owns it.

She owns every one of her decisions: to be a working parent because she loves her job; to only carry two pregnancies because that's all her body can handle; to introduce formula to take away some of the stress of breastfeeding; to schedule regular date nights with her husband; to always have wine on hand.

She owns her dreams: to build a successful, growing occupational therapy business; to adopt a child in the future; to buy a house in the city when so many others are moving away; to have a marriage that impacts others.

She owns her love for her family: putting her three boys before everyone else; setting boundaries to protect their time together; traveling to see their out-of-town family for all major events; honoring her dad's legacy and life with every opportunity.

She owns her love for her friends: showing up for the stuff that counts; praying for them; finding ways to keep connections alive that fit her new lifestyle; inviting her friends into her home, her marriage, and her motherhood—allowing them to love her kids along with her.

The woman just owns it.

But where she's owned it, instead I've questioned, causing me to second-guess myself every step of the way as my insecurities get the better of me.

But she's teaching me an important lesson: if you decide to own it—throwing comparison out the window—you'll gain a freedom that brings joy. Knowing I have plenty of room to grow in the joy department, I'm committed to following her lead, thankful she's paving the way.

Following her example, I'm working towards owning it—*all of it*. Owning my decisions, owning my dreams, owning my love for my family and friends. Owning the things I love; owning the things I hate; owning the things I'm still figuring out. With her hand in mine, I'm going to make no apology for what I care about, what I need help with, where I've fallen down.

I'm learning to own it—the highs and the lows—with no apology.

Frozen

There's this thing little babies do that is my favorite thing in the world. Just as they're starting to wake up, they stretch their little arms and arch their little backs and squint their little eyes and curl up their little legs. And with their little fists framing their little face, they're just a squishy little bundle of joy. And if you pick them up *just then*, they'll remain in this squinty, stretchy, perfectly arched little position as you lift them into your arms.

As if they'll remain frozen in that exact position forever: little, squishy, perfect.

And as you cuddle them close, inhaling their newness and sweetness and so much love, you almost don't notice that they've broken the trance. That the moment is over and they've relaxed into your arms. That they'll soon welcome you into their wakefulness with a smile or a cry or a dirty diaper that needs changing or an empty belly that needs filling.

And just like that, you go from a moment of reveling. Of awe. Of taking in the wonder of their perfect little selves. And you spring into action. Becoming Mom again.

Waiting with bated breath for the next chance to catch them frozen in perfection.

•••••••••••

I stumble down the hallway, feeling my way through the darkness as Micah's cries pierce the night. I open the door and hurry to his bedside. As I reach for him, his arms cling to my neck in desperation, and I let his sweaty cheek find mine.

I swear my heart stops every time his screams jolt me awake. Night terrors are terrifying for all of us.

I carry his shaking body to our chair, a brown leather armchair worn in by love and a history of a child with sleep issues. Fitting solidly into 4T—at the young age of two—my enormous toddler struggles to find a comfortable position in my lap so his mama can hold him and hum him back to sleep.

And for the first time in his young life, I realize I'm running out of room! Too soon he won't fit here.

So as he clings to me, I find myself returning his embrace more tightly than usual. I wrap my arms around his body with the ferocity of a mother realizing that watching your child grow up comes with the requirement of letting them go.

As tears come to my eyes, I sway and hold my now-sleeping baby—no, boy—tight. As if the harder I squeeze the more likely I'll be to stop time, capturing this exact moment of his little-boyhood in my embrace and sealing it in my memory forever. I'm wishing away the turning of time in a desperation familiar to all lovers of tiny humans.

Asking God to keep us frozen here forever—wrapped in the safety of each other's arms.

••••••••••••

In this season with young children, I'm learning to press pause. To intentionally soak in my children. To celebrate the "right now" in the midst of right now's many demands.

To freeze time as only a mother's memory can.

Yet, how many times do I risk missing precious moments with my children for productivity's sake? For impatience's sake? For exhaustion's sake?

How often do I ignore the quiet beckoning of the Lord to pause, to notice, to freeze?

Time is not promised, but I can choose to be intentional with what I have today. I may not be able to freeze it, but I can stop cleaning the kitchen to play cars—again. I can take a deep breath and choose to hug rather than scold. I can watch them sleep as often as I like. I can take countless photos and videos without apology. I can press play on "The Party Freeze Dance Song"—a family favorite—even though we're still in the middle of dinner.

I can choose being together over being put together.

I can and I will.

Deep Breaths

Toddler hiccuping on my lap, we take deep breaths in unison—
Deep breath in.
Deep breath out.
—a calming skill we've been working on together since tantrums started to raise their ugly heads in our house. For us, the body-flinging-on-the-floor charade began at around 18 months, but I just tell myself it's because Micah's advanced for his age.
Deep breath in.
Deep breath out.
I kiss his cheek and he begins to smile.
And just when I think we've finally recovered from our second major meltdown since preschool pickup ninety minutes ago—both his and mine—he wads up his fist and digs his knuckle into my right eyeball socket. Before I can stop him, he's started in on the left.
"Ow! Buddy, what are you doing?!"
"I wipin' your eyes."
"Why, buddy?"
"Because you was crying."
He looks at me with big blue eyes and tear-streaked cheeks.
"You havin' a bad day," he says.
And the corners of my big blue eyes wet again.

"I'm sorry I'm having a bad day, Bubba. Even mamas have bad days sometimes. Can I sing you a song before nap?"

He nods his tousled head and lays it on my shoulder.

As he hugs my neck, I squeeze him with the kind of embrace that only comes after you completely freak out at your children—hoping your fierce touch can communicate the fierce love you're afraid your reactive yelling erased in one fell swoop.

Hug, sing, and hope this is one of those days he won't remember when he grows up.

Deep breath in.

Deep breath out.

Deep breath in.

His breathing slows and I carry his limp body to his bed. Tucking "Puppy" under his elbow, I roll him to his tummy and look upon what's left of his babyhood, fading swiftly from his lean body but hanging on to his cheeks for just a bit longer. I wrap him in his weighted blanket—a worth-every-penny investment for any nap-fighting toddler—and hear him let out a sigh.

Deep breath out.

I exhale a silent prayer over his sleeping soul as I retreat across the wood floor, closing his creaky door with seasoned care.

Deep breath in.

Six hours until bedtime. Four until Daddy gets home.

Time for some coffee.

•••••••••••

Thirty minutes earlier, I was smack dab in the middle of the midday dash. Pick up the kids from school, clean up the breakfast dishes neglected in our race out the door, put something on the table for lunch, clean up the children/table/plates/cookware/floor/ wall after a hurried shared meal with two people still learning how to feed themselves without missing, change a diaper, use the potty, and maybe prep something for dinner before warming a bottle, shutting off the television, and hauling two cranky boys upstairs for a much-needed nap.

Except today there was nothing *dash* about it.

Levi figured out how to pull out the warming drawer on the oven so he could climb up and play with all the buttons on the stove. (And they say you can't tell if your kid is gifted until the preschool years.)

Micah dropped a new roll of toilet paper in a potty full of his own pee—and he was proud of it.

Levi pulled every single spice jar out of the rack and proceeded to bang them on my kitchen floor—leaving red pepper flakes and garlic powder in his wake.

Micah dumped his giant box of Matchbox cars on the family room floor and refused to pick them up. I grabbed his hand and together we shoved those dang backbreakers into their plastic tub as he sobbed, defiant to the very last Corvette.

Levi's breakfast dose of Tylenol lost its battle with his emerging canines.

And after a handful of ineffective time-outs and sharp words, my lack of emotional control peaked as the soggy, urine-soaked roll of toilet paper fell through the thin plastic bag I'd foolishly chosen for its rescue mission and splattered across my floor, my somewhat clean pants, and my curious crawling baby.

Deep breath in.

Closed eyes, fisted hands.

Deep breath out.

Closed-mouth scream. Shaking with fury in the corner.

Pause.

Terrified eyes, reaching hands, wails.

"You scare my ears! Why you do that? Why you be a bear?"

Sometimes my toddler's worldview is so much more accurate than my own. Why would I behave in a way that scares my children? Because I'm a human being with a limit—and mine had been reached, goddangit.

Knowing words wouldn't fix this, I scooped up one boy in each arm, snagged the bottle, and hauled their little sobbing bodies to the second floor for a second chance. Huffing up the stairs with over sixty pounds of crying kids in my arms, I managed to find the empathy that had been missing when I'd lost control and let rage take over.

Deep breath in.

Deep breath out.

We huddled together at the top of the stairs while the baby chugged his formula, quieting first. Leaving him sleeping in his crib, I moved next door with the toddler, and we started the process of calming down together.

Deep breath in.

Deep breath out.

•••••••••••

Kids sound asleep, I return to the scene of the crime, unearthing a new wave of tears. I recount the violence that erupted from my body a half hour ago, and I fight against the shame that threatens to take root.

I rinse my coffee pot.

Deep breath in.

I toss the used grounds in the trash.

Deep breath out.

I reach for my new blend, a seasonal cinnamon spice.

Deep breath in.

I scoop an afternoon's amount into the fresh filter.

Deep breath out.

I close the lid and press ON.

Deep breath in.

The smell of coffee permeates the air.

Deep breath out.

I grab a paper towel, the Thieves cleaner.

Deep breath in.

I kneel and mop up the proof.
Deep breath out.
I throw away the evidence.
Deep breath in.
I pour myself a fresh, warm start.
Deep breath out.
I sit right there on the kitchen floor, tuck my legs beneath me.
Deep breath in.
The rage may be gone, but not yet the regret.

•••••••••••

Daddy arrives home at the promised four-hour mark.
Deep breath in.
I hand him the baby and confess it's been a really bad day. He promises we'll talk about it later and takes his sons to the basement—the basketball hoop beckoning—and gives me a chance to put dinner on the table in peace.
Deep breath out.
I chop the vegetables. I check the chicken. I pull out the plates.

Right here in my kitchen, hurrying to feed my family, I recount the disasters again: the disobedience, my lack of control, my emotional blowout in front of our children. Yet this time, watching my failure highlight reel—regret pressing play in my mind all afternoon—I remember the ending. Instead of only seeing my son's future therapy needs, I recall that after we calmed down a bit, my two-year-old sat on my lap and offered me comfort, "wiping" my tears away with his little hands.

And you know what I realize?

I comfort him more than I yell at him. I hug him more than I lose my patience with him. I speak truth to him more than I speak sharply.

Every day, I love him more than I fail him.

And because of me, he's learning how to love back.

He's learning to respond with tender care when his Mama is

having a bad day because, with every skinned knee and scary dream, he's been met with comfort and love. Every time life has treated him poorly, he's been wrapped in his Mama's arms.

And today I got to see him open his own.

Perhaps my legacy in his life is more love than I realized?

I'm not perfect at this mothering gig—I guarantee I'm less patient than most—but I am confident in one thing: my love is more fierce than my temper.

The oven timer chimes, interrupting my self-reflection. I grab my oven mitts and pull dinner from the oven. I fill plates with roasted chicken smothered in parmesan and garlic. I squeeze a lemon over the still-sizzling meat and cut one portion down to toddler size. I add brown rice with thick pads of Irish butter and dust it with Himalayan salt and fresh-ground pepper. I scoop salads into bowls and sprinkle feta over arugula tossed in oil and balsamic, pinching the last of the lemon. I grab a jar of baby food and a plastic bib, fill a cup with whole milk and snag a bottle of Pellegrino from the garage fridge.

I set each plate in its proper place and open the basement door.

Deep breath in.

"DINNER!"

I hear them storming up the stairs before I see them. Before long, hands are washed and three boys sit around my dinner table. Hands are held and heads are bowed. Daddy says a prayer thanking the Lord for this family, this meal, and this Mama who prepared it.

And in this small moment, I see my love at my table. It's fierce, tender.

Deep breath out.

Peanut Trees

My grandfather is a tall, broad-shouldered man with a full head of white hair and a thick beard that could earn him a seasonal gig as Santa Claus. His large weathered hands are marked by the use he's put them through over the years—physical proof of his lifelong calling to carpentry. "Just like Jesus," he's always said. After the army and a short-lived attempt at a business career, Grandpa Trent said goodbye to the corporate ladder and traded in his business cards for his tool belt and never looked back.

He can usually be seen in jeans and a work shirt, many of them embroidered with a snippet of Scripture or a Bible camp logo. Perhaps his Tilley hat will be on his head, drooping under the weight of all the pins showcasing his life's adventures, each tied to a memory and faded from years on display. On his good days, he's found in his garage woodshop carefully shaping wood into beautiful pieces of furniture, jewelry boxes, or handheld crosses he presents to those he loves. When he greets you with one of his infamous bear hugs, you catch a hint of Old Spice and lingering cigarette smoke. And before he lets you go, he puts his hands on your shoulders, looks you in the eye, takes a deep breath and affirms his love for you. "My granddaughter. How I've missed you."

That's my grandfather. Not another one like him.

When I was a child, there was nothing better than a visit from our grandparents. On each visit, before making his way into the house, my grandfather would sneak to the backyard and carefully place peanuts on the branches of the crabapple tree beside our patio. After formally greeting us at the front door, he'd lead us out back to witness the peanut tree in full bloom, exclaiming with delight that it must be peanut season! Peanut season only occurred when Grandpa was in town—and I swear the surprise never got old. We'd walk under that withering old tree with our eyes turned up to find the treasures he'd hidden for us, not realizing that those peanuts were treasured memories in disguise, ones we'd cherish for years to come.

We'd fill our pockets with our salty treasures, and our hearts would bloom with joy. Life was so beautifully simple back then.

But then, you can't always believe in peanut trees, now can you?

As a direct descendant to that legacy, I'm eternally grateful—even though Grandpa's life hasn't been picture perfect.

Always a person of intention, my grandpa thinks before he speaks, oftentimes pausing for the exact right words. And it seems like the man prays ceaselessly, usually until he's said all he has to say—a practice that antsy family members would lament after long prayer sessions kicking off Christmas dinner. But he's also broken. My grandfather has struggled with bouts of depression that have cost his family in some difficult ways—something usually hidden by the joy he strives to bring into the presence of those he loves most whenever he's able.

But in his imperfect story, what my grandfather has shown me is that while our perfection is not required, our decision to choose faith and pursue joy is. Not only do we need to plant the peanut trees, we must keep our eyes looking upward so we don't miss them coming into bloom.

Today, I'm not sure I have any peanut trees blooming. I'm just a tired mama who's trying to get through the day. And it's been a while since my grandfather has been able to visit to show me the way—he's started to lose feeling in his driving foot due to an ongoing battle with his health only amplified by age. But there's never been a more important season of my life to water the peanut trees. To decide to plant the joy, to look up at it, and take the peace along with me.

In this peanutless season, my boys continue to remind me how purely joyful a child can be—something that feels like ancient history in my own life. And if there's one thing I hope to gift Micah and Levi while miracles are still easy for them to see, it's the joy of the peanut trees. So even though I'm oh so tired, I want to honor my grandfather's pursuit of joy and find chances to plant some peanut trees. I want to leave a legacy of joy that my children will remember for years to come.

I'm sure the magic will still exist—after all, faith only needs a little bit of love to grow.

Spring

Here We Go

*P*erched on the small stool in the gym locker room, I take my first break since the boys woke me before dawn. Blow-drying my hair with one of those travel dryers—like the ones often stowed beneath the sink at a Holiday Inn and also found in my gym bag—I catch a whiff of my burning hair.

Eh, a few lost strands are worth these few minutes to myself.

I just took a shave-your-legs-long shower. My gym bag holds a fresh pair of yoga tights, a well-worn gray hoodie spared from donation for its comfort, and a clean pair of socks.

I take the rare opportunity to slather lotion over my whole body—a practice long forgotten in my busy Mom life—and close my eyes, taking note of my softer curves, my scarred stomach, my sagging, empty breasts. I drink in the scent of lavender and think about the hour before me, already ticking away—and my freedom along with it. I mentally prepare for the day: the short window of time I have to drink some coffee, the quick break for some writing, and the growing packing list for our upcoming vacation—laundry needs piling in response.

I walk into McDonald's and order my medium hot with two creams. I manage to avoid ordering the Egg McMuffin I want. Proud of my self-restraint, I cuddle into my booth with my hot caffeine and my dusty laptop, unravel my ear buds, and press "play." I set the alarm to alert me for the quickly approaching preschool pick-up.

I close my eyes, place my fingers on the keys, and inhale.
Here we go.

•••••••••••

Too quickly, my alarm buzzes, breaking the healing trance that
writing has a habit of creating for my weary soul. I shove the proof
of my freedom into my shoulder bag and toss my paper cup in the
trash, only a couple of drops left.

I push through the heavy glass door and jog, hunched over,
through the parking lot, doing my best to shield my head from the
rain—the weather winning the war against my for-once-dry hair. I
climb in, slam the door, check the clock.

Phew, a few more minutes to myself.

I choose the scenic route to the boys' school. I turn up the volume
on the country station and sing my way into the parking lot.

I use the rare opportunity of arriving early to take a few moments,
before the next phase of my day, to pray—a practice long forgotten in
my busy Mom life—and close my eyes, taking note of my refreshed
mind, my calm spirit, my readiness to squeeze my kids. I relish the
healing trance of pounding rain on my windshield and think about
the hours before me, so quick to start—and my demands along with
them. I mentally prepare for the afternoon: the long window of time
before Daddy gets home, the naptime battle soon to begin, and the
growing packing list for our upcoming vacation—laundry needs
piling in response.

I run out into the wet and key in the code to enter the building.
I manage to avoid catching the eye of my toddler as I run past his
window to scoop up my baby first—his sleepy eyes happy to see
his mama and ready for his crib. I walk next door to his brother's
classroom and am greeted with a bear hug for the record books.

"MOMMY!!"

Baby on my hip and grubby toddler hand clutched in mine, I steel
myself against the rain, and we sprint to the car as fast as we can.

I strap boys into car seats in record time. I climb in and check my rearview mirror, taking note of the two amazing kids I get to call mine.

I close my eyes, pull out my keys, and inhale.

Here we go.

• • • • • • • • • • •

It's a hard afternoon fraught with the demands of a teething baby and his strong-willed older brother, the weather keeping us cooped up and cranky. It's one of those days where the minutes drag at such a slow pace I actually forget to start prepping dinner on time. The sound of the garage door opening—"Daddy's here!"—breaks the trance of *PJ Masks* on the television. I shove a chicken casserole in the oven and turn up the temp. I hand the baby to his father and send them all to the basement to play until it's ready.

After we scarf down a quick dinner, we toss the kids in the bath, then their jammies, then their beds in quick succession. While Dan wipes down the countertops, I load the dishwasher. We scoop up forgotten toys and hide them away in their allotted bins.

Ugh, it's time to start getting ready for bed myself.

I choose the ugly pajamas, their worn holes proof that they're always the right choice after a long day. I wash my face and fill my water glass. I shuffle into our room and flop onto the bed, too tired to adjust the tangled sheets.

I take the rare opportunity of getting in bed on time to talk to my husband without interruption—a practice long forgotten in my busy Mom life—and look him in the eye, telling him about my tired bones, sharing my grateful heart, my desperate need for a good night's sleep. We soak in the comfort of a quiet house—sound machines drumming behind every door—and I think about the hours before me, too few for sure, my exhaustion compounding in their lack. I mentally prepare for tomorrow: the school drop-off, the swim lessons, and the quickly approaching vacation—laundry needs piling in response.

I notice my husband's eyes closing, the familiar hum of his sleeping breath slowing beside me. I roll onto my side and cradle a multitude of pillows. I turn up the volume on the baby monitor.

I close my eyes, say a quick prayer, and exhale.

Here we go.

•••••••••••

Perched on a small stool in our vacation rental, I take my first break since the boys woke me before dawn. Blow-drying my hair with one of those travel dryers—I found it under the sink at our Airbnb—I catch a whiff of my burning hair.

Woo hoo! We're on vacation!

I just took a shave-your-legs-long shower. My beach bag holds a fresh pair of clothes for each person, including a well-worn Cubs hat spared from donation for its comfort, and a pair of flip flops.

I take the rare opportunity to slather sunblock over my whole body—a practice long forgotten in my busy Mom life—and close my eyes, taking note of my softer curves, my scarred stomach, my sagging, empty breasts. I pull on my new one-piece and think about the week before me, already ticking away—and my freedom along with it. I mentally prepare for the return home: the long plane ride with two young kids, the empty refrigerator, and the dirty clothes collecting on our vacation—laundry needs growing in response.

I pause.

No, love. Not yet.

I shift gears.

I walk into the bright kitchen and smile at my family—kids playing with Matchbox cars strewn all over the tile floor and their dad playing referee. While they crash and bang, I pack a cooler of drinks, spread peanut butter on bread. Add the jelly. I manage to avoid eating that extra slice of bacon I want, leftover on the counter from breakfast. Proud of my self-restraint, I carry loads of gear to our rented SUV and help my kids into their suits, their sandals, their car seats. I snag my phone from the counter and walk back into the warm sunny morning.

I shield my eyes, hand the keys to my husband, and inhale.

Here we go.

Spring

She Doesn't Exist

The first time I knew I was a bad mother, my six-month-old had a toilet bowl brush in one hand and a piece of wet, soiled toilet paper dangling from his bottom lip. He had a shit-eating grin on his face.

I hadn't cleaned that toilet in over three weeks.

Of course I hit the panic button and immediately started Googling infant-safe disinfectants to prevent the inevitable life-threatening bacterial infection headed our way by way of one crawling infant's lack of supervision. And I beat myself up about it for days.

He didn't even strike a fever.

The next time my inadequacy was obvious was when I dropped my phone on his face mid-Instagram scroll, and gave him his first semi-black eye when he was supposed to be safely nursing on my lap. Mother of the frickin' year. Try explaining that to your husband without feeling like a terrible person.

Thankfully, the next incident highlighting my failure is less easy to recall.

Call it exhaustion—or just crying "uncle"—but somewhere along this colorful journey of motherhood, I just gave up. I threw my hands in the air and decided to stop keeping track of my failures—because believe me, my list is *way* longer than yours.

And you know what I realized?

She doesn't exist.

She has every nursery rhyme memorized and always buys organic. She doesn't believe toddlers should watch television, and she lost her baby weight before her kid's first round of shots. She can whip up a batch of protein-packed homemade granola bars without looking at a recipe, and she still has time to get those perfect beach waves in her hair. She never misses a workout class and even remembers to give the caregiver at the gym a birthday card. And she knows the caregiver at the gym's birthday!

Come on!

But I promise you, she doesn't exist.

She's filtered. She's 4x4. She's 140 characters.

She's what your own insecurity makes her to be.

Because you know what?

She is SO. FLIPPING. SICK. of Mother Goose. She gets her groceries delivered. Her Mom dropped off those granola bars because she called her in tears the night before when she forgot it was her turn to make the snack for her child's preschool class. Her kid knows every word to that godforsaken Daniel Tiger song. The number on her scale is still higher than she wants it to be and it's been months. She's just making up for the fact that her two-year-old bit that caregiver, and she wants to make sure she doesn't jeopardize the one hour a day she gets some alone time, a workout, the freedom to take a shower without tiny company, and a few spare minutes to actually curl her hair.

And trust me, she's just as tired as you are. And in need of some adult conversation.

Whatever our vision for what motherhood was supposed to be, I'm accepting that it's just a mirage. It doesn't exist.

It's a whole lot messier, isn't it?

It's hard and it's awesome. It's grating and it's revelatory. It costs so much more than the ridiculous price of diapers. It asks more than a toddler who just discovered the brilliance of the word "Why?" It demands more than a little boy who just spotted a blue ball at Target.

It includes a lot of tears—both theirs and mine. And it is nothing like I expected.

But by God's grace, it is so much more.

I am so much more.

And I'm so much more than the lies I believe about my shortcomings.

I only know the baby and toddler chapters in this journey so far. But if my own affection for rebellion—and talking back—in my teenage years is any indication for what's coming my way in a decade or so, this story isn't going to get any easier. And there will be plenty of opportunities for me to contrast my flaws with her alleged perfection.

But every time I swipe, scroll, spy, and stalk, I need to remind myself, she doesn't exist.

She just doesn't exist.

But I do. And I'm more than enough for my family. Even if I'm more hot mess than Mom some days.

Just this past Sunday, we were packing up the car after church—juggling strollers and artwork and a miniature cup of animal crackers that Micah insisted on carrying all the way through the parking lot—and I forgot to buckle the seatbelt on his car seat. We only noticed when he stood up in his chair and leaned out the open window of our moving vehicle. He shoved his little head boldly into the wind, showing off our awesome parenting skills for all the congregation to see.

But he survived.

And I promise, so will you.

Summer

Gorilla Days

I'm so glad I didn't pay close attention to the stories of other families' children growing up. Because they were bound to pale in comparison to seeing the life we created take shape, find a voice, transform into humanity.

What started as a smile, a wave, a crawl, quickly became a word, a hug, first steps. And in a flash, Micah's ordering his own chicken tacos, taking himself to the potty, and shooting baskets in the basement. He can find the letter "M" and sing a blurry version of the ABC's and explain in detail the plot lines of *Paw Patrol*. He can say, "I love you" and ask for another song and give his brother a kiss.

He can also throw himself on the ground at Target and receive a time-out seated in the corner of a public restroom. But hey, you can't win 'em all.

And the surprises keep coming.

This morning a gorilla took residence in our yard. As we walk out the front door, Micah exclaims, "Mama, look! A gorilla! Hurry, hurry. Let's get out of here!" Our Honda Pilot transforms into a Jeep and we drive "Faster, faster!" so the gorilla can't catch us. When I unbuckle him from his car seat upon our arrival at preschool, he grabs my hand and says, "Run!" as we race into the building. The only thing growing faster than his imagination is my affection for him.

Walking back to my car, I smile at the difference one boy, one year, one month, one day can make. These days with Micah, we see more joy than struggle, more fun than tantrum, more sleep than ever before (thank you, children's melatonin). Yet the easier and more joyful life gets, the faster time seems to pass.

Last night, Dan and I couldn't wait for our kids to go to bed—it had been a long and trying evening, ending with Micah refusing dinner, bath, and bed. But as soon as both boys were finally down, we sat side-by-side looking at pictures from a time not so long ago when Micah's cheeks were still chubby and Levi was still just a prayer.

And there was just a hint of grief that came from viewing that slideshow.

My favorite part of having a second baby is getting to start at the beginning again. Because I promise you, the growing up parts went by too fast. This time around, I balance my desperate desire to sleep again with the knowledge that this season is precious, fleeting. I know that there are so many surprises coming. And they're worth the wait, the lack of sleep.

This time, I'm loving Levi with my whole self (and taking just as many pictures). I'm squeezing chunky baby thighs every time the urge hits me, which is often. I'm relishing that his favorite place to be is cradled in my arms. I try to soak up every inch of him as I rock him beyond the start of sleep, just watching him breathe. Thanking the Lord with each quiet moment together.

Because this time I know the truth: *babies don't keep.*

In spite of this knowledge, I still find myself struggling to enjoy certain elements of this season: the exhaustion, the monotony of my days. The difference this time around is that I'm not allowing those frustrations to define me as a mother. When Micah was little, I lost the comparison battle daily, convinced that the mothers around me were free from the negative thoughts I was having about my new role. What I've learned, through honest friendships and self-searching and music and prayer and writing this book, is that I can celebrate the gift of this season—the gift of Levi joining our family—without needing to love every aspect of it. I can savor the parts that bring me deep joy and complain about the parts that suck the life out of me (teething at the top of my current list).

This time, I've freed myself of any expectations about what this season should require of me. I can deeply cherish my boys without smiling through blowouts and temper tantrums and night feedings. I can say it sucks when it sucks.

And most importantly, I can ask for a break.

This time, I'm choosing to accept help from my husband, our mothers, and the wonderful toddler program at Micah's preschool. I'm staying on medication until my hormones feel stable. I'm investing time in the things that give me life: the gym, writing, girls' nights with other moms who keep it real, an occasional date with my husband. Some of these things may take me away from my children, but they return me to them alive, ready to love them from a healthy place.

It hasn't been perfect since Levi's arrival—though it helps that he's genuinely the sweetest baby on earth—but this time, I'm okay that it's not perfect and I'm not perfect at motherhood. And by breaking free from the ideals that once caged me, I've found the contentment that eluded me for quite a while.

This time, I've come to accept the hard days because we also have gorilla days—and I refuse to miss them.

Acknowledgments:

When one sets off to write a book it's never a solo accomplishment. To the fierce tribe that helped me turn this pipe dream into a reality, a most sincere and heartfelt *thank you.*

I will now take this opportunity to write all of my feelings for all of my favorite people as if I was accepting an Oscar.

Here goes...

To my (much-more-private-than-me) husband, Dan, who has stood by my side without ever wavering and rubbed my feet every single day of my pregnancies, thank you for letting me tell our story. Let's hold hands every day.

To Micah and Levi, there is no greater honor than to be your Mom. I love you with every. single. part. of. my. being. But also, please stop peeing on the toilet seat.

To my two biggest fans, Mom and Dad, thank you for always embracing my big personality. My (over) confidence is your doing and it takes a special set of parents to set their kid up to dream without limits. I pray I can give my boys the same gift.

To my sisters, Amy and Katie Claire, I've loved you your whole lives and mine is not complete without you in it. Also, being adult siblings is so much easier, no?

To my in-laws, Danny and Suzi, you two are superheroes. I love being a part of your big, beautiful family and am grateful every day for the son you raised.

To my grandmothers, Barbara and Mary, thank you for paving the way for bold, outspoken women. You continue to bring it. And to my grandfathers, Trent and Bob, I miss you terribly. Your generational impact will live on.

To Ashly Hilst, the woman I paid to give me honest feedback at the very beginning of this process, we did it! You helped this book become a book!

To the team at Köehler for believing in this little memoir of mine and showing me the publishing ropes, I appreciate you! Also, do you think we should look at the cover design again?!

To my therapist who should probably remain unnamed due to HIPAA violations, you were right: a small green pill *is* the difference between life and death. I'm sorry I fought you on that for so many years. Your steadfast investment in my wellbeing has been an eternal gift.

To the many moms I'm privileged to mother among—

Kelly, Katie, Casie, Jessica, Sam, Maddy, Sophie, Martha, Michaja, Sarah R., Colleen, Lauren, Ellen, Emily, Rachel S., Rachel C., Mary, Krista, Megan F., Megan S., Sarah C., Jeniece, Ashley, Kat, Kathryn, Liz, Megan H., Kristin, Vicky, Kimberly, Michelle—

I COULD NOT DO THIS WITHOUT YOU.

To my girlfriends for cheering me on and loving my kids, you are a gift to our lives. To my early readers, your feedback was invaluable. To my book launch team, your participation was huge.

To every person who is still reading this far, thank you for being here. You are loved.